GUIDE TO FOOD STORAGE

Follow this guide for food storage, and you can be sure that what's in your freezer, refrigerator, and pantry is fresh-tasting and ready to use in recipes.

IN THE FREEZER
(At –10° to 0° F)

DAIRY

Cheese, hard	3 months
Cheese, soft	2 weeks
Egg substitute	6 months
Egg whites	6 months
Egg yolks	8 months
Ice cream, sherbet	1 month

FRUITS AND VEGETABLES

Commercially frozen fruits	1 year
Commercially frozen vegetables	8 to 12 months

MEATS, POULTRY, AND SEAFOOD
Beef, Lamb, and Veal

Ground, uncooked, and all cuts, cooked	3 months
Roasts and steaks, uncooked	9 months

Pork

Ground, uncooked, and all cuts, cooked	3 months
Roasts and chops, uncooked	6 months

Poultry

All cuts, cooked	1 month
Boneless or bone-in pieces, uncooked	6 months

Seafood

Bass, perch, trout, and shellfish	3 months
Cod, flounder, and halibut	6 months

IN THE REFRIGERATOR
(At 34° to 40° F)

DAIRY

Buttermilk, low-fat	1 to 2 weeks
Cheese, grated Parmesan	1 year
Cheeses, Cheddar and Swiss	3 to 4 weeks
Cream cheese, ⅓-less-fat, fat-free, and tub-style	2 weeks
Egg substitute, opened	3 days
Fresh eggs in shell	1 month
Milk	7 days

MEATS, POULTRY, AND SEAFOOD
Beef, Lamb, Pork, and Veal

Ground and stew meat, uncooked	1 to 2 days
Roasts, uncooked	2 to 4 days
Steaks and chops, uncooked	3 to 5 days

Chicken, Turkey, and Seafood

All cuts, uncooked	1 to 2 days

FRUITS AND VEGETABLES

Apples, beets, cabbage, carrots, celery, citrus fruits, eggplant, and parsnips	2 to 3 weeks
Apricots, berries, peaches, pears, plums, asparagus, cauliflower, cucumbers, mushrooms, okra, peas, peppers, salad greens, and summer squash	2 to 4 days
Corn, husked	1 day

IN THE PANTRY
Keep these at room temperature for six to 12 months.

BAKING AND COOKING STAPLES
Baking powder
Biscuit and baking mix
Broth, canned
Cooking spray
Honey
Mayonnaise, regular, light, and nonfat (unopened)
Milk, canned evaporated skimmed
Milk, nonfat dry powder
Mustard, prepared (unopened)
Oils, olive and vegetable
Pasta, dried
Peanut butter, reduced-fat
Rice, instant and regular
Salad dressings, bottled (unopened)
Seasoning sauces, bottled
Tuna, canned

FRUITS, LEGUMES, AND VEGETABLES
Fruits, canned
Legumes (beans, lentils, peas), dried or canned
Tomato products, canned
Vegetables, canned

Fresh Tomato, Basil, and Cheese Pizza,
page 85

Shrimp Kebabs with Jalapeño-Lime Marinade, page 76

Texas-Grilled Sirloin with Fresh Tomato Salsa, page 106

**Coconut-Peach Cobbler with
Toasted Pecan Ice Cream, page 50**

Weight Watchers®

Five ★ Star
recipes

Oxmoor House®

©2005 by Oxmoor House, Inc.

Book Division of Southern Progress Corporation

P.O. Box 2262, Birmingham, Alabama 35201-2262

ISBN: 0-8487-3003-8

Library of Congress Control Number: 2005925534

Printed in the United States of America

Second Printing 2005

Be sure to check with your health-care provider before making any changes in your diet.

Weight Watchers® and **POINTS**® are registered trademarks of *Weight Watchers* International, Inc., and are used under license by Healthy Living, Inc.

OXMOOR HOUSE, INC.

Editor in Chief: Nancy Fitzpatrick Wyatt

Executive Editor: Katherine M. Eakin

Art Director: Cynthia Rose Cooper

Copy Chief: Allison Long Lowery

WeightWatchers® **Five-Star Recipes**

Foods Editors: Anne C. Cain, M.S., R.D., L.D.; Alyson M. Haynes

Assistant Foods Editor: Holley C. Johnson, M.S., R.D., L.D.

Copy Editor: Jacqueline Giovanelli

Editorial Assistant: Jessica Dorsey Kohls

Director, Test Kitchens: Elizabeth Tyler Luckett

Assistant Director, Test Kitchens: Julie Christopher

Test Kitchens Staff: Kristi Carter, Nicole Lee Faber,
   Kathleen Royal Phillips, Elise Weis, Kelley Self Wilton

Senior Photographer: Jim Bathie

Senior Photo Stylist: Kay E. Clarke

Photo Stylist: Amy Wilson

Publishing Systems Administrator: Rick Tucker

Director of Production: Phillip Lee

Production Assistant: Faye Porter Bonner

Contributors

Designer: Carol Damsky

Indexer: Mary Ann Laurens

Editorial Intern: Julie Boston

COVER: Chocolate-Strawberry Shortcakes, page 51

To order additional publications, call 1-800-765-6400.

For more books to enrich your life, visit **oxmoorhouse.com**

Contents

Our Best 143 Five-Star Recipes

Eat the foods you love and still lose the weight with **WeightWatchers®** *Five-Star Recipes*, a collection of the best recipes ever published by *Weight Watchers*.

These recipes are staff favorites, the ones that we often prepare for our families and friends. Each recipe has been tested at least twice, often three or four times, to ensure that it's supremely healthy, easy to prepare, and has the all-important "yum factor." This "yum factor" is what elevates a good recipe to "five-star" status. Flavorful ingredients used creatively play an important role, too in these top-rated recipes.

Five-Star Ingredients

Following is our "short list" of flavor-packed ingredients—and some of the recipes in this book that use them—that we often add to an average-tasting recipe to pump up the flavor. Once considered gourmet or hard to find, these ingredients have become staples in our Test Kitchens at work and in our kitchens at home. You should be able to find them in your supermarket.

★ **Balsamic Vinegar** has become the "must-have" ingredient for today's healthy kitchen. The rich, intense flavor quickly transforms simple ingredients into delectable dishes.

- *Grilled Mahimahi Kebabs with Pineapple-Mandarin Sauce, page 68*

- *Spaghetti Squash with White Bean Provençale, page 90*
- *Polenta with Roasted Vegetables, page 91*
- *Raspberry-Balsamic Chicken, page 121*
- *Italian Chicken and Vegetables, page 123*
- *Turkey Cutlets with Balsamic-Brown Sugar Sauce, page 130*
- *White Bean and Tomato Salad, page 146*

★ **Capers** are small grayish green berries that are a common ingredient in Mediterranean cuisine. They're pickled in a vinegar brine or salt-cured, packed in slender glass jars, and can be found with the olives, pickles, and other condiments in the supermarket. A small amount, usually one or two teaspoons, is all you need to add big, bold flavor.

- *Caponata with Garlic Crostini, page 18*
- *Roasted Bell Pepper and Olive Pizzas, page 84*
- *Pasta Puttanesca, page 96*
- *Mediterranean Goat-Cheese Sandwiches, page 178*

★ **Cheese,** with its many types and textures, is a key ingredient in healthy cooking. Fat-free and low-fat cheeses are available, and we use these cheeses successfully in dessert and appetizer recipes. However, for quality and flavor the full-fat cheeses can't be beat. The secret is to add just the right amount to enhance the taste of the food without adding unnecessary fat calories. We use a wide variety of cheeses in recipes. But, if we had to choose one cheese that enhances most recipes, it would be freshly grated Parmesan cheese.

* *Frittata with Swiss Chard, Potatoes, and Fontina, page 86*
* *Roasted Vegetable Macaroni and Cheese, page 94*
* *Double Cheese Meat Loaf, page 100*
* *Greek Feta Chicken, page 122*
* *Mesclun with Caramelized Onion, Apple, and Gruyère Cheese, page 143*
* *Turkey-Havarti Grinder, page 172*

⋆ **Cilantro** is an herb which looks similar to flat-leaf parsley but has a more distinct, lively flavor and aroma. It's generally sold in bunches in the produce section of the grocery store along with parsley. Fresh cilantro adds unique punch to a variety of recipes, whether cooked in the dish or sprinkled on just before serving. It's especially popular in Asian, Caribbean, and Latin American cuisines.

* *Malaysian Lime-Coconut Swordfish, page 72*
* *Beef Tenderloin with Cilantro Sauce, page 105*
* *Texas-Grilled Sirloin with Fresh Tomato Salsa, page 106*
* *Seared Chicken and Peppers with Cilantro Sauce, page 124*
* *Fiery Thai Beef Salad, page 149*
* *Chicken-Mango Wraps, page 171*
* *Spring Posole, page 184*

⋆ **Dark Sesame Oil** is polyunsaturated, making it one of the healthier fats. The sesame seeds are toasted before the oil is pressed, creating a strong, distinct fragrance. A small amount of the oil, usually measured in teaspoonfuls, contributes significant flavor. Dark sesame oil, as well as the milder light sesame oil, are important ingredients in Asian and Indian dishes.

* *Korean-Style Flank Steak, page 105*
* *Oriental Pasta Salad, page 147*
* *Sesame Sugar Snap Peas, page 160*
* *Grilled Marinated Vegetables, page 161*

⋆ **Fresh Ginger or Gingerroot** makes up in flavor for what it lacks in appearance. Beneath the thin skin of this knobby root is one of the most versatile ingredients. As you peel, slice, mince, chop, or grate fresh ginger, a refreshing and spicy aroma fills the air. When used in combination with other ingredients, ginger gives an unmistakable peppery, sweet zing to dishes.

* *Grilled Grouper with Apricot-Ginger Relish, page 66*
* *Grilled Salmon with Ginger-Orange-Mustard Glaze, page 70*
* *Teriyaki Tuna with Fresh Pineapple, page 73*

⋆ **Kalamata Olives** can be found alongside green and black olives in the condiment section of the supermarket. Also known as Greek olives, kalamata olives are packed in olive oil or vinegar. Their pungent, rich, fruity flavor makes them popular in Mediterranean cuisine as an ingredient and as a condiment.

* *Creole Catfish with Vidalia-Olive Relish, page 65*
* *Oven-Poached Halibut Povençale, page 67*
* *Roasted Lemon Chicken with Potatoes, page 128*

About Our Recipes

WeightWatchers® *Five-Star Recipes* gives you the nutrition facts you need to make your life easier. We've provided the following useful information with every recipe:

★ A number calculated through the **POINTS®** Food System (a component of the **POINTS** Weight-Loss System) from *Weight Watchers* International, Inc.

★ Diabetic exchange values for those who use them as a guide for planning meals

★ A complete nutrient analysis per serving

POINTS Food System

Every recipe in the book includes a number calculated using the **POINTS** Food System. This system uses a formula based on the calorie, fat, and fiber content of the food. Foods with more calories and fat (like a slice of pepperoni pizza) receive high numbers, while fruits and vegetables receive low numbers. For more information about the *Weight Watchers* program and a meeting nearest you, call 1-800-651-6000 or go to www.weightwatchers.com.

Diabetic Exchanges

We provide exchange values for people who use them for calorie-controlled diets and for people with diabetes. All foods within a certain group contain approximately the same amount of nutrients and calories, so one serving of a food from a food group can be substituted or exchanged for one serving of any other item on the list. The food groups are starch, vegetable, fruit, milk, meat, and fat. The exchange values are based on the *Exchange Lists for Meal Planning* developed by the American Diabetes Association and The American Dietetic Association.

Nutrient Analysis

Each recipe has a complete list of nutrients, including calories, fat, saturated fat, protein, carbohydrate, dietary fiber, cholesterol, iron, sodium, and calcium. Measurements are abbreviated g (grams) and mg (milligrams). Numbers are based on these assumptions:

- Unless otherwise indicated, meat, poultry, and fish refer to skinned, boned, and cooked servings.
- When we give a range for an ingredient (3 to 3½ cups flour, for instance), we calculate using the lesser amount.
- Some alcohol calories evaporate during heating; the analysis reflects that.
- Only the amount of marinade absorbed by the food is used in calculation.
- Garnishes and optional ingredients are not included in an analysis.

Nutritional values used in our calculations either come from The Food Processor, Version 7.5 (ESHA Research) or are provided by food manufacturers.

Appetizers
&
Beverages

THREE-PEPPER SALSA

This spicy salsa is for those who can take the heat. Serve with baked tortilla chips or as a flavorful sauce to dress up plain grilled fish fillets or chicken breasts.

POINTS value:
0

exchanges:
1 vegetable

per serving:
Calories 26
Fat 0.4g (saturated fat 0.1g)
Protein 1g
Carbohydrate 5.6g
Fiber 1.5g
Cholesterol 0mg
Iron 0.6mg
Sodium 79mg
Calcium 12mg

1½ cups boiling water
3 ancho chiles or ½ teaspoon crushed red pepper
2 large poblano chiles
1 large yellow bell pepper
1 cup diced tomato
½ cup diced red onion
¼ cup chopped fresh cilantro
3 tablespoons orange juice
2 tablespoons fresh lime juice
2 tablespoons minced seeded serrano chile
¼ teaspoon salt

1. Combine boiling water and ancho chiles in a small bowl; cover and let stand 30 minutes or until soft. Drain well; seed and chop.
2. Preheat broiler.
3. While anchos soak, cut poblanos and bell pepper in half lengthwise; discard seeds and membranes. Place poblanos and bell pepper halves, skin sides up, on a foil-lined baking sheet; flatten with hand. Broil 10 minutes or until blackened. Place in a zip-top plastic bag; seal. Let stand 10 minutes. Peel and dice poblanos and bell pepper.
4. Combine anchos, roasted poblanos and bell pepper, tomato, and remaining ingredients in a medium bowl; stir well. Cover and chill until ready to serve. Yield: 9 servings (serving size: ¼ cup).

Taming the Heat: One of the best ways to tame a chile pepper's heat is to remove the chile's seeds and membranes, which hold most of the heat-inducing capsaicin. If your mouth is on fire from eating a hot chile pepper, drink some milk or eat a slice of bread to neutralize the burning sensation.

PINEAPPLE-CHIPOTLE SALSA

Chipotle chiles and adobo sauce provide a wonderful smoky essence
for this fruit salsa. It's ideal with fish or grilled pork tenderloin.

2	teaspoons vegetable oil
3	cups diced fresh pineapple or canned pineapple tidbits
1½	cups diced onion
1	cup diced seeded tomato
2	garlic cloves, minced
½	cup pineapple juice
2	tablespoons brown sugar
2	tablespoons cider vinegar
2	drained canned chipotle chiles in adobo sauce, minced
1	tablespoon adobo sauce (from chipotle chiles)
½	cup chopped fresh cilantro
2	tablespoons fresh lime juice
½	teaspoon salt

POINTS value:
1

exchanges:
½ fruit
1 vegetable

per serving:
Calories 63
Fat 1.3g (saturated fat 0.2g)
Protein 0.8g
Carbohydrate 13.4g
Fiber 1.6g
Cholesterol 0mg
Iron 0.6mg
Sodium 129mg
Calcium 19mg

1. Heat oil in a large nonstick skillet over medium-high
heat. Add pineapple and onion; sauté 10 minutes or until
lightly browned. Add tomato and garlic; sauté 1 minute.
Stir in pineapple juice, brown sugar, vinegar, chiles, and
adobo sauce. Cook 6 minutes, stirring occasionally. Stir in
cilantro, lime juice, and salt. Serve warm or, if desired, cover
and chill. Yield: 10 servings (serving size: ¼ cup).

Pineapple Pointers: A ripe pineapple will be deep
golden brown in color and will have a slightly sweet smell; it will
also be a bit soft to the touch. You will be able to pull out the
leaves from the top without much effort. To store fresh pineapple,
refrigerate, tightly wrapped, for 2 to 3 days. If it's slightly
underripe, you can keep it at room temperature for a couple of
days—it will become less acidic, but not necessarily sweeter.

HUMMUS WITH RASPBERRY VINEGAR

pictured on page 21

Raspberry vinegar gives this hummus a fruity twist, but you can use any kind of vinegar you have on hand. Serve with pita wedges and crisp, raw vegetables for a colorful, healthy appetizer. Enjoy it the next day as an afternoon snack.

POINTS value:
1

exchanges:
½ starch

per serving:
Calories 44
Fat 1.3g (saturated fat 0.2g)
Protein 1.9g
Carbohydrate 6.6g
Fiber 1g
Cholesterol 0mg
Iron 0.6mg
Sodium 75mg
Calcium 14mg

1   tablespoon olive oil
1½ cups diced onion
2   tablespoons raspberry vinegar
1   (15½-ounce) can chickpeas (garbanzo beans), undrained
1   tablespoon chopped fresh cilantro
½   teaspoon ground cumin
½   teaspoon coarsely ground black pepper
¼   teaspoon salt
Cilantro sprigs (optional)

1. Heat oil in a nonstick skillet over medium-high heat. Add onion, and sauté 5 minutes or until onion begins to brown. Add vinegar; bring to a boil, and cook 2 minutes or until vinegar evaporates. Cool to room temperature.
2. While onion mixture cools, drain chickpeas through a sieve over a bowl, reserving ¼ cup liquid. Place chickpeas and chopped cilantro in a food processor, and process until mixture resembles coarse meal. Add onion mixture, ¼ cup reserved liquid, cumin, pepper, and salt; process until smooth. Spoon into a bowl. Garnish with cilantro sprigs, if desired. Yield: 16 servings (serving size: 2 tablespoons).

CREAMY GUACAMOLE

This Mexican dip features ricotta cheese, which makes it creamy and decreases the fat by extending the avocado. Serve with baked tortilla chips.

1½ cups cubed peeled avocado (about 2 avocados)
1 cup fat–free ricotta cheese
⅓ cup coarsely chopped onion
2 tablespoons coarsely chopped fresh cilantro
2 tablespoons fresh lime juice
1 tablespoon coarsely chopped seeded jalapeño pepper
½ teaspoon salt

1. Place all ingredients in a food processor; process until smooth. Serve immediately. Yield: 20 servings (serving size: 2 tablespoons).

About Avocados: Avocados are available year-round. To select a ripe one, press lightly on the skin, and feel the flesh yield to the pressure. The flesh will quickly turn brown when exposed to air, so don't cut an avocado until just before serving or using in a recipe. An avocado is actually a fruit, but because of its buttery texture, rich flavor, and high fat content, it's usually categorized as a fat. The good news is that more than half of its fat is monounsaturated—the fat that is believed to have health benefits.

POINTS value:
1

exchanges:
½ vegetable

per serving:
Calories 30
Fat 1.7g (saturated fat 0.3g)
Protein 1.3g
Carbohydrate 2.3g
Fiber 1g
Cholesterol 2mg
Iron 0.1mg
Sodium 73mg
Calcium 22mg

PARTY SPINACH DIP

Perfect for game-day munchies, this appetizer can be made ahead and chilled until ready to serve. Offer an assortment of crackers, breadsticks, Melba toast, or raw vegetables for dippers.

POINTS value:
0

exchanges:
1 vegetable

per serving:
Calories 25
Fat 0.8g (saturated fat 0.5g)
Protein 2.4g
Carbohydrate 2.3g
Fiber 0.5g
Cholesterol 3mg
Iron 0.3mg
Sodium 130mg
Calcium 27mg

1 (12-ounce) carton 1% low-fat cottage cheese
1 (10-ounce) package frozen chopped spinach, thawed, drained, and squeezed dry
½ cup low-fat sour cream
¼ cup dry vegetable soup mix
2 teaspoons grated fresh onion
1 teaspoon lemon juice
1 (8-ounce) can sliced water chestnuts, drained and chopped

1. Place cottage cheese in a food processor, and process until smooth, scraping sides of bowl once. Place in a medium bowl.
2. Stir spinach and remaining ingredients into cheese. Cover and chill until ready to serve. Yield: 24 servings (serving size: 2 tablespoons).

Double Dippers: Here's a variety of dippers with low **POINTS** values.

	POINTS value
*2 low-sodium saltine crackers	0
*2 whole-grain Melba snack crackers	0
*2 short crunchy breadsticks	1
*2 (½-inch-thick) slices French baguette	1

prep: 5 minutes ★ **cook:** 10 minutes

TEX-MEX BLACK BEAN DIP

You can't beat this crowd-pleasing dip. Serve warm or at room temperature with fat-free baked tortilla chips or homemade flour tortilla chips (recipe in box below).

1	teaspoon vegetable oil
½	cup chopped onion
2	garlic cloves, minced
1	(15-ounce) can black beans, drained
½	cup diced tomato
⅓	cup mild picante sauce
½	teaspoon ground cumin
½	teaspoon chili powder
¼	cup (1 ounce) shredded reduced-fat Monterey Jack cheese
¼	cup chopped fresh cilantro
1	tablespoon fresh lime juice

POINTS value:
1

exchanges:
½ starch

per serving:
Calories 42
Fat 1g (saturated fat 0.4g)
Protein 2.6g
Carbohydrate 6.2g
Fiber 1g
Cholesterol 2mg
Iron 0.6mg
Sodium 136mg
Calcium 30mg

1. Heat oil in a medium nonstick skillet over medium heat. Add onion and garlic; sauté 4 minutes or until tender. Add beans, tomato, and next 3 ingredients; cook 5 minutes or until thick, stirring constantly. Remove from heat; add cheese, cilantro, and lime juice, stirring until cheese melts. Yield: 13 servings (serving size: 2 tablespoons).

Homemade Tortilla Chips: Cut (6-inch) flour tortillas into 6 wedges each, and toast in a 350° oven for 8 to 10 minutes or until lightly browned. Six chips have a **POINTS** value of 2.

CAPONATA WITH GARLIC CROSTINI

A great make-ahead recipe, the zesty caponata will keep in the refrigerator for one to two days. Bring it to room temperature before serving.

POINTS value:
3

exchanges:
1½ starch
1 vegetable
1 fat

per serving:
Calories 174
Fat 3.8g (saturated fat 0.6g)
Protein 4.9g
Carbohydrate 31.4g
Fiber 3.2g
Cholesterol 0mg
Iron 1.6mg
Sodium 552mg
Calcium 44mg

1	tablespoon olive oil
4	cups diced eggplant (about 1 pound)
1	cup coarsely chopped Vidalia or other sweet onion
½	cup diced red bell pepper
½	cup diced yellow bell pepper
1	garlic clove, minced
1	tablespoon brown sugar
2	tablespoons fresh lemon juice
½	teaspoon salt
¼	cup golden raisins
2	tablespoons capers
1	tablespoon pine nuts, toasted
2	tablespoons chopped fresh basil
24	(½-inch-thick) slices diagonally cut French bread baguette (about 10 ounces)
1	garlic clove, halved

Olive oil-flavored cooking spray

1. Preheat oven to 375°.

2. Heat oil in a large nonstick skillet over medium-high heat. Add eggplant, onion, bell peppers, and minced garlic; sauté 5 minutes. Stir in sugar, lemon juice, and salt; cook 1 minute. Stir in raisins, capers, and pine nuts. Place eggplant mixture in a large bowl; stir in basil.

3. Place bread slices on a baking sheet. Bake at 375° for 7 minutes or until toasted. Rub cut sides of garlic clove over 1 side of each bread slice. Coat bread slices with cooking spray, and bake an additional 2 minutes. Serve caponata with crostini. Yield: 8 servings (serving size: ⅓ cup caponata and 3 crostini).

prep: 12 minutes ★ **cook:** 12 minutes

SANTA FE CHICKEN QUESADILLAS

These quesadillas are cut into appetizer-size wedges—ideal finger food for a party. Let your guests add their own salsa so the wedges don't get soggy.
A whole quesadilla is a quick entrée with a **POINTS** value of 4.

1¼ cups salsa, divided
1   cup chopped cooked chicken breast
2   tablespoons chopped fresh cilantro
1   teaspoon ground cumin
1   (4.5-ounce) can chopped green chiles, drained
6   (7-inch) flour tortillas
1   cup (4 ounces) shredded reduced-fat sharp Cheddar cheese
Cooking spray

1. Combine ½ cup salsa, chicken, and next 3 ingredients. Spoon mixture evenly onto 1 half of each tortilla. Sprinkle with cheese.

2. Coat a nonstick skillet with cooking spray; place over medium-high heat until hot. Add 1 tortilla; cook 1 minute. Fold in half; cook 30 seconds. Turn quesadilla over; cook 30 seconds. Repeat with remaining tortillas. Cut each into 4 wedges. Serve with ¾ cup salsa. Yield: 24 servings (serving size: 1 wedge and 1½ teaspoons salsa).

POINTS value:
1

exchanges:
½ starch
½ very lean meat

per serving:
Calories 61
Fat 1.9g (saturated fat 0.7g)
Protein 4.6g
Carbohydrate 6.3g
Fiber 0.3g
Cholesterol 9mg
Iron 0.5mg
Sodium 238mg
Calcium 63mg

Precooked Chicken: If you're using precooked chicken in a recipe, here are some substitution amounts that will be useful:

Type	Cup Measures
1 pound uncooked skinless, boneless chicken	3 cups chopped cooked chicken
1 (5.5-ounce) skinless, boneless chicken breast half	1 cup chopped cooked chicken
1 (2-pound) uncooked chicken	2¼ cups chopped cooked chicken
1 (2-pound) rotisserie chicken	3 to 3½ cups chopped chicken
1 (6-ounce) package grilled chicken strips	1⅓ cups chopped cooked chicken
1 (9-ounce) package frozen chopped cooked chicken	1⅔ cups chopped cooked chicken

BUFFALO SHRIMP WITH BLUE CHEESE DIP

You're going to love this creamy homemade dip. With a **POINTS** value of
1 per 2-tablespoon serving, it makes a great salad dressing, too.

POINTS value:
1

exchanges:
1 lean meat

per serving:
Calories 62
Fat 0.8g (saturated fat 0.3g)
Protein 10.6g
Carbohydrate 2.7g
Fiber 0.1g
Cholesterol 83mg
Iron 1.4mg
Sodium 189mg
Calcium 34mg

48   unpeeled large shrimp (about 2 pounds)
2   tablespoons dark brown sugar
2   tablespoons chopped onion
3   tablespoons cider vinegar
2   tablespoons water
2   tablespoons ketchup
1   tablespoon Worcestershire sauce
2   to 4 teaspoons hot sauce
¼   teaspoon pepper
1   garlic clove, chopped
¾   cup fat-free cottage cheese
3   tablespoons fat-free milk
2   tablespoons crumbled blue cheese
⅛   teaspoon pepper
Cooking spray

1. Peel shrimp, leaving tails intact. Place shrimp in a shallow dish; cover and chill.
2. Place sugar and next 8 ingredients in a blender; process until smooth. Pour mixture into a small saucepan. Cook 10 minutes over medium-low heat, stirring occasionally. Cool 1 hour; pour over shrimp. Cover and marinate in refrigerator 30 minutes, turning shrimp occasionally.
3. While shrimp marinate, place cottage cheese and next 3 ingredients in blender; process until smooth. Spoon into a bowl. Cover; chill until shrimp are ready.
4. Prepare grill or preheat broiler.
5. Remove shrimp from dish, reserving marinade. Arrange shrimp in a single layer on a grill rack or broiler pan coated with cooking spray. Cook 3 minutes; turn shrimp over, and baste with reserved marinade. Cook 3 minutes or until shrimp are done. Serve with cheese dip. Yield: 16 servings (serving size: 3 shrimp and 1 tablespoon dip).

Hummus with Raspberry Vinegar, page 14

**Berry Refresher,
page 26**

Buttermilk Pancakes, page 32

**Banana-Oatmeal Bread,
page 34**

prep: 5 minutes ★ cook: 2 minutes

COFFEE ROYALE

For a nonalcoholic version, omit the amaretto; increase the coffee to 3¼ cups.

1¼ cups 1% low-fat milk
1   tablespoon sugar
¼   teaspoon ground cinnamon
2¾   cups hot strong brewed coffee
½   cup amaretto (almond-flavored liqueur)

1. Combine first 3 ingredients in a medium saucepan. Place over medium heat, and cook 2 minutes or until sugar dissolves, stirring constantly. Remove from heat; stir in coffee and amaretto. Pour into mugs; serve warm. Yield: 6 servings (serving size: ¾ cup).

POINTS **value:**
2

exchanges:
½ starch
½ low-fat milk

per serving:
Calories 96
Fat 0.6g (saturated fat 0.4g)
Protein 1.8g
Carbohydrate 10.9g
Fiber 0g
Cholesterol 2mg
Iron 0.5mg
Sodium 28mg
Calcium 66mg

---

prep: 3 minutes ★ cook: 15 minutes ★ other: 1 hour

CIDER TEA

2   cups apple cider
2   cups water
¼   cup sugar
4   whole allspice
4   whole cloves
4   regular-size red zinger tea bags

1. Combine first 5 ingredients in a large saucepan; let stand 1 hour. Bring to a boil. Add tea bags; remove from heat. Cover and steep 10 minutes. Pour tea through a wire-mesh strainer into mugs, discarding spices and tea bags. Serve warm. Yield: 4 servings (serving size: 1 cup).

POINTS **value:**
2

exchanges:
1½ starch

per serving:
Calories 107
Fat 0.1g (saturated fat 0g)
Protein 0.1g
Carbohydrate 27g
Fiber 0.1g
Cholesterol 0mg
Iron 0.5mg
Sodium 4mg
Calcium 9mg

prep: 8 minutes

BERRY REFRESHER
pictured on page 22

POINTS value:
2

exchanges:
1½ fruit
½ fat-free milk

per serving:
Calories 128
Fat 1.1g (saturated fat 0.6g)
Protein 3.6g
Carbohydrate 27g
Fiber 1.4g
Cholesterol 3mg
Iron 0.3mg
Sodium 41mg
Calcium 115mg

1   cup halved fresh strawberries
2   tablespoons powdered sugar
1   (8-ounce) container raspberry low-fat yogurt
½   (6-ounce) can thawed orange juice concentrate, undiluted
10   ice cubes

1. Place all ingredients in a blender; process until smooth. Serve immediately. Yield: 3 servings (serving size: 1 cup).

prep: 2 minutes ★ other: 1 hour

CHERRY LIMEADE

POINTS value:
3

exchanges:
2 starch

per serving:
Calories 149
Fat 0g (saturated fat 0g)
Protein 0.1g
Carbohydrate 35g
Fiber 0g
Cholesterol 0mg
Iron 0.2mg
Sodium 18mg
Calcium 21mg

1   (6-ounce) jar maraschino cherries with stems
1   (6-ounce) can thawed limeade concentrate, undiluted
1   cup water
2   cups lime-flavored sparkling water, chilled

1. Drain cherries, reserving ⅓ cup juice. Set aside 8 cherries, reserving remaining cherries for another use.
2. Combine ⅓ cup cherry juice, limeade concentrate, and 1 cup water in a pitcher. Cover and chill at least 1 hour.
3. Just before serving, stir in sparkling water. Serve immediately with cherries over crushed ice. Yield: 4 servings (serving size: 1 cup limeade and 2 cherries).

Breads

prep: 5 minutes ★ **cook:** 45 minutes ★ **other:** 30 minutes

POPOVERS

Leavened with steam and eggs, these miniature "bread balloons" are crusty on the outside and almost hollow on the inside. If you don't have a popover pan, use a muffin pan, and bake the popovers for about 30 to 35 minutes.

POINTS value:
3

exchanges:
1 starch
1 fat

per serving:
Calories 141
Fat 5g (saturated fat 2.1g)
Protein 5.6g
Carbohydrate 18.1g
Fiber 0.6g
Cholesterol 78mg
Iron 1.2mg
Sodium 257mg
Calcium 48mg

1   cup all-purpose flour
½   teaspoon salt
1   cup 1% low-fat milk
2   large eggs
1   tablespoon butter, melted
Cooking spray
1   teaspoon vegetable oil

1. Preheat oven to 375°.
2. Lightly spoon flour into a dry measuring cup; level with a knife. Combine flour and salt, stirring with a whisk. Combine milk and eggs in a bowl, stirring with a whisk until blended; let stand 30 minutes. Gradually add flour mixture, stirring well with a whisk. Stir in butter.
3. Coat 9 popover cups with cooking spray; brush oil evenly among cups to coat. Place popover pan in a 375° oven for 5 minutes. Divide batter evenly among prepared popover cups. Bake at 375° for 40 minutes or until golden. Serve immediately. Yield: 9 servings (serving size: 1 popover).

Popover Pointers: Although it's tempting, don't open the oven door to peek at the popovers. Instead, use the oven light, and view through the glass to see when they're done. Popovers should be golden and crispy on the outside and soft on the inside; undercooked ones are pale on the outside and gummy on the inside. When done, the interior of a popover should be somewhat hollow and moist. Popovers "deflate" quickly, so serve them immediately.

CHEDDAR DROP BISCUITS

These savory cheese biscuits, brushed with parsley-garlic butter, will become a dinnertime favorite. They're super easy to make and their flavor is outstanding.

2   cups low-fat baking mix (such as reduced-fat Bisquick)
½   cup (2 ounces) shredded reduced-fat sharp Cheddar cheese
¾   cup fat-free milk
Cooking spray
2   tablespoons light butter, melted
½   teaspoon dried parsley, crushed
¼   teaspoon garlic powder

POINTS value:
2

exchanges:
1 starch
½ fat

per serving:
Calories 106
Fat 3.5g (saturated fat 1g)
Protein 3.4g
Carbohydrate 15g
Fiber 0.3g
Cholesterol 3mg
Iron 0.7mg
Sodium 291mg
Calcium 76mg

1. Preheat oven to 450°.
2. Lightly spoon baking mix into a dry measuring cup; level with a knife. Combine baking mix and cheese in a bowl; make a well in center of mixture. Add milk, stirring just until moist.
3. Drop dough by rounded tablespoonfuls, 2 inches apart, onto a baking sheet coated with cooking spray. Bake at 450° for 8 to 10 minutes or until biscuits are golden.
4. Combine butter, parsley, and garlic powder in a small bowl; brush over warm biscuits. Serve immediately. Yield: 12 servings (serving size: 1 biscuit).

Drop Biscuit Basics: Because drop biscuits have a higher proportion of liquid to dry ingredients than rolled biscuits, you'll have a thick batter instead of a soft dough. That's why it's necessary to "drop" the dough by tablespoonfuls onto a baking sheet coated with cooking spray.

TART CHERRY AND VANILLA SCONES

Brighten up a cold winter day with a scone and a hot cup of tea. For cranberry scones, substitute ¾ cup dried cranberries for the tart cherries, and bake as directed.

POINTS value:
5

exchanges:
2 starch
½ fruit
1 fat

per serving:
Calories 247
Fat 6.3g (saturated fat 1.4g)
Protein 4.8g
Carbohydrate 43g
Fiber 2g
Cholesterol 1mg
Iron 2.2mg
Sodium 211mg
Calcium 109mg

¾ cup dried tart cherries
¼ cup boiling water
1¾ cups all-purpose flour
⅓ cup sugar
¼ cup yellow cornmeal
2 teaspoons baking powder
¼ teaspoon salt
2 tablespoons chilled butter, cut into small pieces
2 tablespoons vegetable shortening
⅓ cup plain fat-free yogurt
¼ cup evaporated fat-free milk
1 teaspoon vanilla extract
¼ teaspoon butter extract
Cooking spray
1 large egg white, lightly beaten
2 teaspoons sugar

1. Combine cherries and boiling water in a bowl; cover and let stand 10 minutes or until softened. Drain and set aside.
2. Preheat oven to 400°.
3. Lightly spoon flour into dry measuring cups; level with a knife. Combine flour and next 4 ingredients in a large bowl; cut in butter and shortening with a pastry blender or 2 knives until mixture resembles coarse meal.
4. Combine cherries, yogurt, milk, and extracts; add to flour mixture, stirring just until moist (dough will be sticky). Turn dough out onto a lightly floured surface, and lightly knead 4 times with floured hands.
5. Pat dough into an 8-inch circle on a baking sheet coated with cooking spray. Brush egg white over dough, and sprinkle with 2 teaspoons sugar. Cut dough into 8 wedges, cutting into but not through dough.
6. Bake at 400° for 18 minutes or until golden. Serve warm. Yield: 8 servings (serving size: 1 scone).

BLUEBERRY-YOGURT MUFFINS

These muffins are about as satisfying and versatile as a food can be.
They harmonize perfectly with coffee and the morning paper, with a salad
for a light lunch, or with milk as a snack anytime.

2	cups all-purpose flour
⅓	cup sugar
1	teaspoon baking powder
1	teaspoon baking soda
¼	teaspoon salt
¼	cup orange juice
2	tablespoons vegetable oil
1	teaspoon vanilla extract
1	large egg, lightly beaten
1	(8-ounce) carton vanilla low-fat yogurt
1	cup fresh or frozen blueberries, thawed

Cooking spray

1	tablespoon sugar

POINTS value:
3

exchanges:
1½ starch
½ fat

per serving:
Calories 150
Fat 3.4g (saturated fat 0.7g)
Protein 3.5g
Carbohydrate 26.4g
Fiber 1.1g
Cholesterol 19mg
Iron 1mg
Sodium 161mg
Calcium 69mg

1. Preheat oven to 400°.
2. Lightly spoon flour into dry measuring cups; level with a knife. Combine flour and next 4 ingredients in a large bowl; make a well in center of mixture. Combine orange juice and next 4 ingredients; add to flour mixture, stirring just until moist. Gently fold in blueberries.
3. Spoon batter evenly into 12 muffin cups coated with cooking spray; sprinkle 1 tablespoon sugar evenly over batter. Bake at 400° for 18 minutes or until a wooden pick inserted in center comes out clean. Remove from pans immediately; cool on a wire rack. Yield: 12 servings (serving size: 1 muffin).

BUTTERMILK PANCAKES
pictured on page 23

Nothing can surpass the welcoming aroma of pancakes hot off the griddle. We've given you the **POINTS** value per pancake to help you plan your serving size. One tablespoon maple syrup has a **POINTS** value of 1.

POINTS value:
2

exchanges:
1 starch

per serving:
Calories 92
Fat 2.6g (saturated fat 0.8g)
Protein 3g
Carbohydrate 14g
Fiber 0.3g
Cholesterol 25mg
Iron 0.7mg
Sodium 102mg
Calcium 19mg

1   cup all-purpose flour
2   tablespoons sugar
1   teaspoon baking powder
½   teaspoon baking soda
1   cup low-fat buttermilk
1   tablespoon vegetable oil
1   large egg, lightly beaten
Maple syrup (optional)

1. Lightly spoon flour into a dry measuring cup; level with a knife. Combine flour, sugar, baking powder, and baking soda in a large bowl; stir with a whisk. Combine buttermilk, oil, and egg; add to flour mixture, stirring until batter is smooth.

2. Spoon about ¼ cup batter per pancake onto a hot nonstick griddle or nonstick skillet. Turn pancakes when tops are covered with bubbles and edges look cooked. Serve with maple syrup, if desired. Yield: 9 pancakes (serving size: 1 pancake).

Perfect Pancakes:
When cooking pancakes, flip them over when the top surface is full of bubbles. The underside will be golden.

prep: 15 minutes ★ **cook:** 1 hour

BROCCOLI CORN BREAD

To make an extra pan of corn bread to freeze and have on hand for later, use
the whole package of broccoli and double the rest of the ingredients.
Serve with a bowl of hot vegetable soup.

Cooking spray
1   tablespoon light butter
½   (10-ounce) package frozen chopped broccoli, thawed
    and drained
1   (8½-ounce) package corn muffin mix
1   (2-ounce) jar diced pimiento, drained
¾   cup 1% low-fat cottage cheese
½   cup finely chopped onion
½   cup egg substitute
¼   teaspoon cracked pepper

1. Preheat oven to 350°.
2. Coat an 8-inch square pan with cooking spray. Add
butter to pan, and place in heated oven for 3 minutes or
until butter melts.
3. Press broccoli between paper towels to remove excess
moisture. Combine broccoli, muffin mix, and next
5 ingredients in a bowl; stir well. Pour batter into prepared
pan. Bake at 350° for 1 hour or until golden. Yield: 16
servings (serving size: 1 square).

POINTS **value:**
2

exchanges:
½ starch
½ vegetable
½ fat

per serving:
Calories 82
Fat 2.2g (saturated fat 0.7g)
Protein 3.4g
Carbohydrate 12.2g
Fiber 0.9g
Cholesterol 0mg
Iron 0.7mg
Sodium 186mg
Calcium 15mg

prep: 15 minutes ★ **cook:** 1 hour and 10 minutes ★ **other:** 1 hour and 10 minutes

BANANA-OATMEAL BREAD
pictured on page 24

We took banana bread to the next yummy level with the addition of chewy oats, brown sugar, and a hint of cinnamon. Serve warm for breakfast, or pack a slice with your lunch for an afternoon snack.

POINTS value:
4

exchanges:
1½ starch
½ fruit
1 fat

per serving:
Calories 185
Fat 6.1g (saturated fat 1.2g)
Protein 3.3g
Carbohydrate 30.1g
Fiber 1.3g
Cholesterol 12mg
Iron 1.3mg
Sodium 200mg
Calcium 72mg

1   cup packed brown sugar
7   tablespoons vegetable oil
2   large egg whites
1   large egg
1   cup regular oats
1⅓ cups mashed ripe banana (about 2 large)
½   cup fat-free milk
2   cups all-purpose flour
1   tablespoon baking powder
½   teaspoon baking soda
½   teaspoon salt
½   teaspoon ground cinnamon
Cooking spray

1. Preheat oven to 350°.
2. Combine first 4 ingredients in a large bowl; beat with a mixer at medium speed until blended. Combine oats, banana, and milk; add to sugar mixture, beating well.
3. Lightly spoon flour into dry measuring cups; level with a knife. Combine flour, baking powder, baking soda, salt, and cinnamon; stir with a whisk. Add to sugar mixture; beat just until moist.
4. Spoon batter into a 9 x 5-inch loaf pan coated with cooking spray. Bake at 350° for 1 hour and 10 minutes or until a wooden pick inserted in center comes out clean. Cool 10 minutes in pan on a wire rack; remove loaf from pan. Cool completely on wire rack. Yield: 18 servings (serving size: 1 slice).

No-Knead Bread

If you love wholesome, homemade yeast bread but don't have much time,
this is your recipe. It requires no kneading or shaping and you
end up with 3 beautiful loaves.

3   packages dry yeast (about 6¾ teaspoons)
3¾ cups warm water (100° to 110°)
10 cups all-purpose flour
6   tablespoons sugar
1   tablespoon salt
6   tablespoons butter, melted
2   large eggs, lightly beaten
Cooking spray

POINTS value:
2

exchanges:
1½ starch

per serving:
Calories 111
Fat 1.9g (saturated fat 0.4g)
Protein 2.9g
Carbohydrate 20.1g
Fiber 0.8g
Cholesterol 9mg
Iron 1.2mg
Sodium 166mg
Calcium 6mg

1. Dissolve yeast in warm water in a large bowl, and let
stand 5 minutes.

2. Lightly spoon flour into dry measuring cups; level with
a knife. Add flour and next 4 ingredients to yeast mixture,
stirring until well blended. Cover and let rise in a warm
place (85°), free from drafts, 30 minutes or until doubled in
size. (Press two fingers into dough. If indentation remains,
the dough has risen enough.) Spoon dough evenly into
3 (9 x 5-inch) loaf pans coated with cooking spray. Let
dough rise 20 minutes or until doubled in size.

3. Preheat oven to 350°.

4. Bake at 350° for 40 minutes or until loaves sound
hollow when tapped. Remove from pans; cool on wire racks.
Yield: 3 loaves, 16 servings per loaf (serving size: 1 slice).

When time permits, there's nothing more therapeutic
than kneading dough for homemade bread. But some days simply
don't allow for leisurely baking. That's why we've offered a
variety of yeast bread recipes. When you have time for making
"from-scratch" yeast bread, try Classic Breadsticks (page 36) or
Oatmeal-Raisin Bread (page 38). When you need to take a few
shortcuts, go for No-Knead Bread (recipe above) that goes
straight from the batter bowl to the loaf pans for rising or
Parmesan-Onion Rolls (page 37) that start with a hot roll mix.

CLASSIC BREADSTICKS

POINTS value:
2

exchanges:
1 starch
½ fat

per serving:
Calories 106
Fat 2.2g (saturated fat 0.3g)
Protein 3.9g
Carbohydrate 17.6g
Fiber 0.8g
Cholesterol 0mg
Iron 1.4mg
Sodium 129mg
Calcium 47mg

3 cups bread flour
¼ cup nonfat dry milk
1 teaspoon salt
1 teaspoon sugar
2 teaspoons olive oil
1 package quick-rise yeast (about 2¼ teaspoons)
1 cup plus 2 tablespoons very warm water (120° to 130°)
Cooking spray
1 tablespoon cornmeal
1 large egg white, lightly beaten
1 tablespoon water

1. Lightly spoon flour into dry measuring cups; level with a knife. Place flour and next 5 ingredients in a food processor; pulse 6 times or until blended. With processor on, slowly add very warm water through food chute, and process until dough forms a ball. Process 1 additional minute. Turn dough out onto a floured surface; knead lightly 4 to 5 times.

2. Place dough in a large bowl coated with cooking spray, turning to coat top. Cover dough, and let rise in a warm place (85°), free from drafts, 40 minutes or until doubled in size. (Press two fingers into dough. If indentation remains, the dough has risen enough.)

3. Coat 2 baking sheets with cooking spray; sprinkle each with 1½ teaspoons cornmeal, and set aside.

4. Punch dough down; turn out onto a floured surface. Divide dough into 20 equal portions, shaping each portion into a 12-inch rope. Place ropes 2 inches apart on baking sheets. Cover ropes, and let rise 20 minutes or until puffy.

5. Preheat oven to 400°.

6. Uncover dough. Combine egg white and 1 tablespoon water, and gently brush over breadsticks.

7. Bake at 400° for 15 minutes or until lightly browned. Remove from pans; cool on wire racks. Yield: 20 servings (serving size: 1 breadstick).

PARMESAN-ONION ROLLS

Cooking spray
¾   cup finely chopped onion
½   teaspoon dried oregano
½   teaspoon dried basil
1   (16-ounce) box hot roll mix
1   cup very warm water (120° to 130°)
2   tablespoons butter, softened
1   large egg white, lightly beaten
1   cup (4 ounces) grated fresh Parmesan cheese

1. Place a nonstick skillet coated with cooking spray over medium-high heat until hot. Add onion, oregano, and basil; sauté until onion is tender. Set aside.

2. Combine contents of roll mix box and enclosed yeast packet in a large bowl; stir well. Add very warm water, butter, and egg white, stirring until dough pulls away from sides of bowl. Turn dough out onto a lightly floured surface. Sprinkle with onion mixture; knead until blended. Sprinkle dough with cheese; knead 5 minutes or until dough is smooth and elastic. Place bowl over dough to cover; let rest 10 minutes.

3. Divide dough into 16 equal portions. Shape each portion into a ball. Place 8 balls in each of 2 (8-inch) round cake pans coated with cooking spray. Cover; let rise in a warm place (85°), free from drafts, 25 minutes or until doubled in size.

4. Preheat oven to 375°.

5. Uncover dough. Bake at 375° for 20 minutes or until lightly browned. Serve warm. Yield: 16 servings (serving size: 1 roll).

POINTS value:
3

exchanges:
1½ starch
1 fat

per serving:
Calories 156
Fat 5g (saturated fat 2.1g)
Protein 6g
Carbohydrate 21.5g
Fiber 0.2g
Cholesterol 10mg
Iron 0.3mg
Sodium 249mg
Calcium 109mg

OATMEAL–RAISIN BREAD

POINTS value:
2

exchanges:
1½ starch

per serving:
Calories 121
Fat 0.7g (saturated fat 0.1g)
Protein 3.5g
Carbohydrate 25.4g
Fiber 0.8g
Cholesterol 0mg
Iron 1.3mg
Sodium 197mg
Calcium 9mg

4   cups bread flour, divided
1   cup very warm water (120° to 130°)
1   package dry yeast (about 2¼ teaspoons)
½   cup regular oats
¾   cup boiling water
1   cup raisins
3   tablespoons honey
½   teaspoon ground cinnamon
2   teaspoons salt
1   teaspoon cider vinegar
Cooking spray

1. Lightly spoon bread flour into dry measuring cups; level with a knife. Combine ¾ cup bread flour, very warm water, and yeast in a large bowl; stir well with a whisk. Cover and let stand at room temperature 1 hour.
2. Combine oats and boiling water in a small bowl. Stir in raisins, honey, and cinnamon; cool.
3. Add 3¼ cups bread flour, salt, and vinegar to yeast mixture. Add oat mixture; stir until a soft dough forms (dough will feel tacky). Turn dough out onto a lightly floured surface. Knead dough until smooth and elastic (about 10 to 12 minutes). Shape into 2 (8-inch) oval loaves. Make 3 parallel cuts ¼-inch-deep across tops of loaves using a sharp knife. Place loaves on a baking sheet coated with cooking spray. Spray tops with cooking spray. Cover and let rise in a warm place (85°), free from drafts, 30 minutes or until doubled in size. (Gently press two fingers into dough. If indentation remains, the dough has risen enough.)
4. Preheat oven to 375°.
5. Uncover dough. Bake at 375° for 30 minutes or until loaves sound hollow when tapped. Remove from pan; cool on a wire rack. Yield: 24 servings (serving size: 1 slice).

Desserts

STUFFED POACHED PEARS
pictured on facing page

Ideal for entertaining, this upscale dessert can be made in the morning and chilled until your guests are ready for dessert.

POINTS value:
5

exchanges:
1 starch
2 fruit
1 fat

per serving:
Calories 251
Fat 6g (saturated fat 0.7g)
Protein 3.4g
Carbohydrate 51.5g
Fiber 6g
Cholesterol 0mg
Iron 1.7mg
Sodium 24mg
Calcium 41mg

4	large Bosc pears
1	cup water
1	cup dry white wine
2	tablespoons sugar
2	tablespoons honey
4	dried apricots
2	(3 x ½-inch) lemon rind strips
1	whole clove
1	teaspoon vanilla extract
4	reduced-calorie vanilla wafers, crushed
5	tablespoons coarsely chopped pistachios, almonds, or walnuts, toasted and divided

1. Peel pears and core from the bottom, leaving stems intact. Slice about ¼ inch from base of each pear so it will sit flat.

2. Combine water and next 7 ingredients in a large saucepan; bring to a boil. Add pears; cover, reduce heat, and simmer 10 minutes or until tender. Remove pears and apricots from cooking liquid, using a slotted spoon; chill pears and apricots at least 2 hours. Bring cooking liquid to a boil; cook until reduced to 1 cup (about 15 minutes). Strain cooking liquid through a sieve over a bowl; discard solids. Chill.

3. Chop apricots. Combine apricots, wafer crumbs, and 1 tablespoon pistachios. Stuff about 2 tablespoons apricot mixture into each pear cavity. Place 1 pear in each of 4 bowls. Spoon syrup over each pear; sprinkle each with pistachios. Yield: 4 servings (serving size: 1 pear, ¼ cup syrup, and 1 tablespoon pistachios).

Note: Use a melon baller to core pears.

Stuffed Poached Pears

Mocha-Chocolate Cheesecake,
page 52

**Oatmeal-Raisin Cookies,
page 58**

Chocolate-Strawberry Shortcakes, page 51

DARK-CHOCOLATE SOUFFLÉ CAKE

Cooking spray

¾ cup water

½ cup granulated sugar

½ cup packed dark brown sugar

1 tablespoon instant espresso or 2 tablespoons instant coffee granules

⅔ cup Dutch process or unsweetened cocoa

¼ teaspoon salt

2 ounces semisweet chocolate, chopped

2 ounces unsweetened chocolate, chopped

2 tablespoons Kahlúa (coffee-flavored liqueur), coffee-flavored syrup, or strong brewed coffee

3 large egg yolks

⅓ cup sifted cake flour

6 large egg whites

¼ teaspoon cream of tartar

⅓ cup granulated sugar

POINTS value:

4

exchanges:

2 starch

1 fat

per serving:

Calories 196

Fat 6g (saturated fat 3.2g)

Protein 4.9g

Carbohydrate 33.6g

Fiber 0.3g

Cholesterol 55mg

Iron 1.9mg

Sodium 84mg

Calcium 29mg

1. Coat bottom of a 9-inch springform pan with cooking spray. Set aside.

2. Combine water, ½ cup granulated sugar, ½ cup brown sugar, and espresso in a large saucepan; bring to a boil, stirring until sugar dissolves. Remove from heat; add cocoa, salt, and chopped chocolates, stirring with a whisk until chocolate melts. Stir in Kahlúa and egg yolks. Lightly spoon flour into a dry measuring cup; level with a knife. Stir in flour until well blended; cool to room temperature. Set aside.

3. Preheat oven to 300°.

4. Beat egg whites and cream of tartar with a mixer at high speed until foamy. Add ⅓ cup granulated sugar, 1 tablespoon at a time, beating until stiff peaks form. Gently fold one-fourth of egg white mixture into chocolate mixture; gently fold in remaining egg white mixture, adding one-fourth mixture at a time. Spoon into prepared pan. Bake at 300° for 1 hour or until a wooden pick inserted in center comes out almost clean. Cool completely on a wire rack. Remove sides from pan. Yield: 12 servings (serving size: 1 wedge).

APPLE–OATMEAL CRUMB CAKE

Sweet bits of apple appear throughout this tender crumb cake. Not only is it a top choice for dessert, but it's delicious for breakfast, brunch, and snacks, too.

POINTS value:
4

exchanges:
1½ starch
½ fruit
1 fat

per serving:
Calories 204
Fat 6.9g (saturated fat 1.4g)
Protein 3.1g
Carbohydrate 33g
Fiber 1.3g
Cholesterol 28mg
Iron 1.2mg
Sodium 154mg
Calcium 33mg

1   cup all-purpose flour
⅓   cup regular oats
⅓   cup granulated sugar
⅓   cup packed dark brown sugar
⅛   teaspoon salt
⅛   teaspoon ground nutmeg
¼   cup chilled butter, cut into small pieces
½   teaspoon baking powder
¼   teaspoon baking soda
⅓   cup apple juice
1   teaspoon vanilla extract
1   large egg
1½ cups coarsely chopped peeled McIntosh apple (about 2 apples)
Cooking spray

1. Preheat oven to 350°.

2. Lightly spoon flour into a dry measuring cup, and level with a knife. Combine flour and next 5 ingredients in a bowl; cut in butter with a pastry blender or 2 knives until mixture resembles coarse meal. Reserve ½ cup flour mixture for topping; set aside.

3. Combine remaining flour mixture, baking powder, and baking soda; add apple juice, vanilla extract, and egg. Beat mixture at medium speed of a mixer until blended; fold in chopped apple.

4. Spoon batter into an 8-inch round cake pan coated with cooking spray, and sprinkle reserved ½ cup flour mixture over batter. Bake at 350° for 30 minutes or until cake springs back when touched lightly in center. Cool cake on a wire rack. Yield: 8 servings (serving size: 1 wedge).

prep: 25 minutes ★ cook: 1 hour ★ other: 1 hour and 10 minutes

LEMON-POPPY SEED POUND CAKE

Cooking spray
1   teaspoon all-purpose flour
1   cup granulated sugar
⅓   cup butter, softened
2   large egg whites
1   large egg
1   tablespoon grated lemon rind
1   teaspoon vanilla extract
1⅔ cups all-purpose flour
2   tablespoons poppy seeds
1   teaspoon baking powder
¼   teaspoon baking soda
⅛   teaspoon salt
¾   cup low-fat buttermilk
⅔   cup powdered sugar
4   teaspoons fresh lemon juice

POINTS value:
5

exchanges:
2 starch
1½ fat

per serving:
Calories 226
Fat 6.7g (saturated fat 3.6g)
Protein 3.8g
Carbohydrate 38.2g
Fiber 0.6g
Cholesterol 32mg
Iron 1.1mg
Sodium 166mg
Calcium 70mg

1. Preheat oven to 350°.

2. Coat an 8 x 4-inch loaf pan with cooking spray; dust with 1 teaspoon flour. Set aside.

3. Beat granulated sugar and butter with a mixer at medium speed until well blended (about 4 minutes). Add egg whites and egg, 1 at a time, beating well after each addition. Beat in lemon rind and vanilla.

4. Lightly spoon 1⅔ cups flour into dry measuring cups; level with a knife. Combine 1⅔ cups flour and next 4 ingredients, stirring well with a whisk. Add flour mixture to sugar mixture alternately with buttermilk, beginning and ending with flour mixture.

5. Pour batter into prepared pan. Bake at 350° for 1 hour or until a wooden pick inserted in center comes out clean. Cool in pan 10 minutes on a wire rack; remove from pan. Poke holes in top of cake using a skewer. Combine powdered sugar and lemon juice in a small bowl; brush over warm cake. Cool completely. Yield: 12 servings (serving size: 1 slice).

CAPPUCCINO ANGEL CAKE

POINTS value:
3

exchanges:
2 starch

per serving:
Calories 161
Fat 1.3g (saturated fat 0.7g)
Protein 3.6g
Carbohydrate 35g
Fiber 0.3g
Cholesterol 0mg
Iron 0.3mg
Sodium 279mg
Calcium 48mg

1 (16-ounce) package angel food cake mix
1¼ cups cold water
¼ cup semisweet chocolate minichips
2 tablespoons instant coffee granules

1. Preheat oven to 350°.
2. Beat cake mix and water in a large bowl with a mixer at low speed 30 seconds. Beat at medium speed 1 minute. Gently fold in chocolate chips and coffee granules (coffee will not dissolve). Spoon batter into an ungreased 10-inch tube pan, spreading evenly. Break air pockets by cutting through batter with a knife.
3. Bake at 350° for 37 minutes or until cake springs back when touched lightly. Invert pan onto a heatproof glass bottle, and cool upside down in pan. Loosen cake from sides of pan using a narrow metal spatual or knife. Invert cake onto a plate. Yield: 12 servings (serving size: 1 slice).

Tips for Heavenly Angel Cake:
• Break air pockets by cutting through batter with a knife.
• Use the correct pan size.
• Bake immediately after preparing the batter.
• Check accuracy of oven temperature with a thermometer.
• Do not underbake.
• Cool cake upside down in pan on a heatproof glass bottle in an area free from drafts.

EASY CARAMEL–BANANA TART

Instead of soaking the raisins in rum, you may substitute 2 tablespoons water and ⅛ teaspoon rum extract. If you don't have golden raisins on hand, black raisins will work fine.

¼   cup golden raisins
2   tablespoons dark rum
½   (15-ounce) package refrigerated pie dough (such as Pillsbury)
Cooking spray
3   cups (¼-inch-thick) diagonally sliced ripe banana (about 1½ pounds)
6   tablespoons caramel ice cream topping

1. Combine raisins and rum in a small bowl; set aside.
2. Preheat oven to 425°.
3. Roll dough into a 10½-inch circle, and place on a foil-lined baking sheet coated with cooking spray. Arrange banana slices in concentric circles on crust, leaving a 2-inch border. Fold 2-inch border of dough over banana slices, pressing gently to seal (dough will partially cover slices). Bake at 425° for 30 minutes.
4. Place caramel topping in a microwave-safe bowl. Microwave at HIGH 20 seconds or until warm. Stir in raisin mixture. Pour over banana slices. Cut into 6 wedges. Yield: 6 servings (serving size: 1 wedge).

POINTS value:
7

exchanges:
½ starch
2 fruit
2 fat

per serving:
Calories 315
Fat 9.5g (saturated fat 4g)
Protein 3.3g
Carbohydrate 53g
Fiber 2.2g
Cholesterol 6.6mg
Iron 0.3mg
Sodium 178mg
Calcium 37mg

prep: 40 minutes ★ **cook:** 35 minutes ★ **other:** 2 hours

COCONUT–PEACH COBBLER WITH TOASTED PECAN ICE CREAM

pictured on page 4

POINTS value:
7

exchanges:
2 starch
2 fruit
1 fat

per serving:
Calories 306
Fat 8.7g (saturated fat 4g)
Protein 5.9g
Carbohydrate 53.3g
Fiber 0.9g
Cholesterol 45mg
Iron 1.6mg
Sodium 223mg
Calcium 136mg

4   cups vanilla low-fat ice cream, softened
¼   cup chopped pecans, toasted
2   cups all-purpose flour
3   tablespoons granulated sugar
1   tablespoon baking powder
¼   teaspoon salt
½   cup flaked sweetened coconut, toasted
6   tablespoons chilled butter, cut into small
     pieces
½   cup evaporated fat-free milk
2   large egg yolks
11 cups sliced peeled peaches (about 4 pounds)
1   cup packed brown sugar
6   tablespoons all-purpose flour
¼   teaspoon ground nutmeg
⅛   teaspoon salt
Cooking spray
1   tablespoon granulated sugar

1. Combine ice cream and pecans in a bowl; stir well. Cover and freeze at least 1 hour.
2. Lightly spoon 2 cups flour into dry measuring cups, and level with a knife. Place 2 cups flour, 3 tablespoons granulated sugar, baking powder, and ¼ teaspoon salt in a food processor, and pulse 2 times or until blended. Add coconut and butter, and pulse 10 times or until mixture resembles coarse meal. Combine milk and egg yolks. Remove 1 tablespoon milk mixture; set aside. With processor on, slowly pour remaining milk mixture through food chute; pulse 5 times or just until blended. Press mixture gently into a 6-inch square on heavy-duty plastic wrap; cover with additional plastic wrap. Chill at least 30 minutes. Roll dough, still covered, into a 14 x 10-inch rectangle.
3. Preheat oven to 350°.
4. Combine peaches, brown sugar, 6 tablespoons flour, nutmeg, and ⅛ teaspoon salt in a large bowl; spoon into a

13 x 9-inch baking dish coated with cooking spray.
Remove 1 sheet of plastic wrap from dough; place dough
on peach mixture, pressing to edge of dish. Remove
remaining sheet of plastic wrap; brush dough with reserved
milk mixture. Cut 6 (2-inch) slits in dough; sprinkle with
1 tablespoon granulated sugar. Bake at 350° for 35 minutes
or until golden. Let stand 30 minutes on a wire rack. Spoon
¼ cup ice cream over each serving. Yield: 16 servings.

prep: 8 minutes ★ **other:** 5 minutes

CHOCOLATE-STRAWBERRY SHORTCAKES
pictured on page 44 and cover

There's no baking involved in this recipe, thanks to a few good convenience products.
The fudgy cookies soak up the juice from the strawberries.

2   cups sliced strawberries
1   tablespoon granulated sugar
8   sugar-free chocolate brownie cookies (such as
    Snackwell's)
1   cup frozen reduced-calorie whipped topping,
    thawed
¼   cup fat-free hot fudge topping
Powdered sugar (optional)

1. Combine strawberries and granulated sugar in a bowl.
Stir gently to dissolve sugar; let stand 5 minutes.
2. Spoon ¼ cup strawberries onto each of 4 serving plates.
Place 1 cookie on top of strawberries; top each cookie
with 2 tablespoons whipped topping. Divide remaining
strawberries evenly over whipped topping; spoon remaining whipped topping evenly over strawberries. Top with
remaining 4 cookies.
3. Spoon fudge topping into a small heavy-duty zip-top
plastic bag. Microwave at HIGH 20 seconds or just until
softened. Snip a small hole in corner of bag; drizzle fudge
topping evenly over shortcakes. Sprinkle with powdered
sugar, if desired. Yield: 4 servings (serving size: 1 shortcake).

POINTS **value:**
6

exchanges:
2½ starch
1 fruit
1 fat

per serving:
Calories 308
Fat 9.3g (saturated fat 4g)
Protein 3.6g
Carbohydrate 60.5g
Fiber 2.2g
Cholesterol 0mg
Iron 2.9mg
Sodium 296mg
Calcium 33.3mg

MOCHA-CHOCOLATE CHEESECAKE
pictured on page 42

We used low-fat sour cream, fat-free cream cheese, and reduced-fat cream cheese to get a cheesecake that weighs in with half the **POINTS** value of its full-fat counterpart.

POINTS value:
5

exchanges:
2 starch
1 lean meat
1 fat

per serving:
Calories 251
Fat 7.7g (saturated fat 2.2g)
Protein 10.5g
Carbohydrate 33.7g
Fiber 1.2g
Cholesterol 46mg
Iron 1.1mg
Sodium 304mg
Calcium 110mg

1 cup reduced-fat cream-filled chocolate sandwich cookies (such as reduced-fat Oreos; about 11 cookies)
2 tablespoons sugar
1 tablespoon butter, melted
Cooking spray
3 (8-ounce) blocks fat-free cream cheese, softened
1 (8-ounce) block ⅓-less-fat cream cheese, softened
1¼ cups sugar
½ cup low-fat sour cream
⅓ cup Kahlúa (coffee-flavored liqueur) or coffee-flavored syrup
½ cup Dutch process cocoa or unsweetened cocoa
3 tablespoons all-purpose flour
2 large eggs
2 large egg whites
2 teaspoons vanilla extract
1 cup frozen fat-free whipped topping, thawed
16 chocolate-coated coffee beans, crushed

1. Preheat oven to 325°.

2. Combine first 3 ingredients in a bowl; toss with a fork until moist. Press mixture into bottom of a 9-inch springform pan coated with cooking spray.

3. Beat cream cheeses and 1¼ cups sugar with a mixer at high speed until creamy. Add sour cream and Kahlúa; beat just until blended. Add cocoa and flour; beat just until blended. Add eggs and egg whites, 1 at a time, beating just until blended after each addition. Stir in vanilla.

4. Pour batter into prepared pan. Bake at 325° for 1 hour or until almost set. Cheesecake is done when center barely moves when pan is touched. Remove from oven; run a knife around outside edge. Cool to room temperature. Cover and chill at least 8 hours. Top each slice with 1 tablespoon whipped topping and 1 crushed chocolate-coated coffee bean. Yield: 16 servings (serving size: 1 wedge).

prep: 15 minutes ★ **cook:** 35 minutes ★ **other:** 1 hour

LEMON–MERINGUE SURPRISE PIE

The "surprise" in this pie is tofu, a true "superfood." In addition to its health benefits, tofu helps create a silky, smooth filling for this pie.

1	cup firm tofu (about 7 ounces)
1	teaspoon grated lemon rind
⅓	cup fresh lemon juice
1½	cups water
1	cup sugar
⅓	cup cornstarch
2	large egg yolks, lightly beaten
1	(9-inch) reduced-fat graham cracker crust (such as Keebler)
3	large egg whites
¼	teaspoon cream of tartar
⅛	teaspoon salt
⅓	cup sugar

POINTS value:
6

exchanges:
3 starch
1 fat

per serving:
Calories 292
Fat 5.5g (saturated fat 1.6g)
Protein 5g
Carbohydrate 55.8g
Fiber 1.2g
Cholesterol 54mg
Iron 1.9mg
Sodium 156mg
Calcium 34mg

1. Preheat oven to 325°.

2. Place first 3 ingredients in a blender; process until smooth. Combine water, 1 cup sugar, and cornstarch in a medium saucepan. Bring to a boil; cook 1 minute or until thick, stirring constantly with a whisk. Gradually add sugar mixture to egg yolks in a bowl, stirring constantly with a whisk. Pour yolk mixture into pan. Bring to a boil over medium heat; cook 1 minute, stirring constantly. Remove from heat, and stir in tofu mixture. Spread filling mixture evenly into crust.

3. Beat egg whites, cream of tartar, and salt with a mixer at high speed until foamy. Gradually add ⅓ cup sugar, 1 tablespoon at a time, beating until stiff peaks form. Spread evenly over warm filling, sealing to edge of crust. Bake at 325° for 25 minutes; cool pie 1 hour on a wire rack. Cut with a sharp knife dipped in hot water. Yield: 8 servings (serving size: 1 wedge).

ALMOND RICE PUDDING

POINTS value:
5

exchanges:
2½ starch
1 fat

per serving:
Calories 239
Fat 5.5g (saturated fat 1.8g)
Protein 6.9g
Carbohydrate 44.3g
Fiber 0.6g
Cholesterol 10mg
Iron 1.2mg
Sodium 96mg
Calcium 174mg

1¼ cups water
3   tablespoons light butter
1   (3-inch) cinnamon stick
1   cup uncooked long-grain rice
3   cups fat-free milk, divided
⅔   cup sugar
¼   cup nonfat dry milk
1   teaspoon vanilla extract
4   teaspoons cinnamon-sugar
8   teaspoons chopped almonds

1. Bring first 3 ingredients to a boil in a medium saucepan. Stir in rice; cover, reduce heat to medium-low, and simmer 10 minutes or until liquid is absorbed. Stir in 1 cup milk and sugar; cook, uncovered, 10 minutes or until liquid is nearly absorbed, stirring frequently. Add 1 cup milk and dry milk; cook, uncovered, 10 minutes or until liquid is nearly absorbed, stirring frequently. Add ½ cup milk; cook, uncovered, 15 minutes or until liquid is nearly absorbed, stirring constantly. Add remaining ½ cup milk; cook until rice is tender and mixture is thick and creamy. Remove from heat; stir in vanilla. Serve warm or chilled topped with cinnamon-sugar and chopped almonds. Yield: 8 servings (serving size: ½ cup pudding, ½ teaspoon cinnamon-sugar, and 1 teaspoon almonds).

STRAWBERRY ICE CREAM

This decadent ice cream gets its creaminess and cheesecake-like flavor from cream cheese and sweetened condensed milk. It's sure to be a family favorite.

2½ cups 1% low-fat milk, divided
2   large egg yolks
½   cup (4 ounces) block-style ⅓-less-fat cream cheese,
     cubed and softened
3   cups finely chopped strawberries
1   tablespoon fresh lime juice
1   tablespoon vanilla extract
1   (14-ounce) can fat-free sweetened condensed milk

1. Combine 1¼ cups low-fat milk and egg yolks in a small, heavy saucepan; stir well with a whisk. Heat to 180° or until tiny bubbles form around edge of pan, stirring frequently (do not boil). Remove from heat. Add cream cheese, stirring until smooth. Combine cream cheese mixture, 1¼ cups low-fat milk, strawberries, and remaining ingredients in a large bowl; stir until well blended. Cover and chill completely.

2. Pour mixture into the freezer can of an ice-cream freezer, and freeze according to manufacturer's instructions. Spoon ice cream into a freezer-safe container; cover and freeze 2 hours or until firm. Yield: 9½ cups, 19 servings (serving size: ½ cup).

POINTS value:
2

exchanges:
½ starch
½ low-fat milk
½ fat

per serving:
Calories 104
Fat 2.4g (saturated fat 1.3g)
Protein 3.7g
Carbohydrate 16.5g
Fiber 0.6g
Cholesterol 30mg
Iron 0.2mg
Sodium 62mg
Calcium 103mg

PINEAPPLE–BROWN SUGAR FROZEN YOGURT

POINTS value:
3

exchanges:
1 starch
½ low-fat milk

per serving:
Calories 142
Fat 0.7g (saturated fat 0.4g)
Protein 2.7g
Carbohydrate 32.4g
Fiber 0.4g
Cholesterol 3mg
Iron 0.5mg
Sodium 41mg
Calcium 109mg

¾ cup packed light brown sugar
1 (15¼-ounce) can crushed pineapple in juice, undrained
2 cups vanilla low-fat yogurt
1 teaspoon vanilla extract

1. Combine sugar and pineapple with juice in a medium saucepan over medium heat; cook until sugar dissolves, stirring occasionally. Remove from heat, and cool slightly. Chill.
2. Combine pineapple mixture, yogurt, and vanilla in a large bowl. Pour mixture into the freezer can of an ice-cream freezer, and freeze according to manufacturer's instructions. Spoon yogurt into a freezer-safe container; cover and freeze 1 hour or until firm. Yield: 9 servings (serving size: ½ cup).

Frozen Facts: Before you use your ice-cream freezer, read the manufacturer's instructions carefully. Freezers are made of different materials, and this makes a difference in the recommended ice-salt ratio. Don't skimp on the ice and salt; they're essential for proper freezing. The yogurt and ice cream freeze because their heat is absorbed by the ice and salt. Ice alone isn't cold enough to freeze yogurt or ice cream. If you use too little salt, the brine won't get cold enough to freeze yogurt or ice cream. With too much salt, yogurt and ice cream will freeze too quickly, causing large ice crystals to form. Rock salt is preferred over table salt because rock salt is slower to dissolve.

PUFFED-UP CHOCOLATE-CHIP COOKIES

This is one of the best chocolate-chip cookies you'll ever make—and it doesn't scrimp on chocolate. Applesauce is the secret to these moist treats.

½ cup applesauce
1¼ cups all-purpose flour
1½ teaspoons baking powder
¾ teaspoon salt
1 cup packed brown sugar
¼ cup butter, softened
1 tablespoon vanilla extract
1 large egg
1 cup semisweet chocolate chips
Cooking spray

1. Preheat oven to 375°.
2. Spoon applesauce into a fine sieve over a bowl, and let stand 15 minutes.
3. While applesauce drains, lightly spoon flour into dry measuring cups; level with a knife. Combine flour, baking powder, and salt in a small bowl; stir well with a whisk.
4. Discard liquid from applesauce. Scrape drained applesauce into a large bowl. Add sugar and butter; beat with a mixer at medium speed until light and fluffy (about 2 minutes). Beat in vanilla and egg. Add flour mixture; beat at low speed until well blended. Fold in chips.
5. Drop dough by level tablespoons 2 inches apart onto baking sheets coated with cooking spray. Bake at 375° for 10 minutes or until almost set. Cool on pans 2 to 3 minutes or until firm. Remove cookies from pans; cool on wire racks. Store cookies in an airtight container at room temperature. Yield: 3 dozen (serving size: 1 cookie).

POINTS value:
2

exchanges:
1 starch

per serving:
Calories 78
Fat 2.9g (saturated fat 1.7g)
Protein 0.8g
Carbohydrate 12.8g
Fiber 0.2g
Cholesterol 10mg
Iron 0.5mg
Sodium 87mg
Calcium 20mg

OATMEAL-RAISIN COOKIES
pictured on page 43

To ensure moistness, use fresh raisins that are plump and soft.

POINTS value:
2

exchanges:
1 starch
½ fat

per serving:
Calories 101
Fat 3.1g (saturated fat 1.7g)
Protein 1.5g
Carbohydrate 17.3g
Fiber 0.6g
Cholesterol 16mg
Iron 0.6mg
Sodium 43mg
Calcium 10mg

½   cup granulated sugar
½   cup packed brown sugar
⅓   cup butter, softened
1   teaspoon vanilla extract
⅛   teaspoon salt
1   large egg
1   cup all-purpose flour
1   cup regular oats
½   cup raisins
Cooking spray

1. Preheat oven to 350°.
2. Beat first 6 ingredients with a mixer at medium speed until light and fluffy. Lightly spoon flour into a dry measuring cup, and level with a knife. Add flour and oats to egg mixture; beat until blended. Stir in raisins.
3. Drop by level tablespoons 2 inches apart onto baking sheets coated with cooking spray. Bake at 350° for 15 minutes or until golden brown. Cool on pans 3 minutes. Remove cookies from pans; cool on wire racks. Yield: 2 dozen (serving size: 1 cookie).

Easy Measuring: Measure the first few spoonfuls of dough with a tablespoon from your measuring spoon set so you can gauge the correct amount of dough, then increase your speed with this two-spoon technique:
1. With one spoon (from your flatware), pick up the same amount of dough.
2. With the other spoon, push the dough off onto the baking sheet.

FUDGY CHOCOLATE BROWNIES

When you add the cocoa and sugar to the melted chocolate, the mixture forms a ball that's hard to stir. Don't worry—once the mixture has cooled slightly and the eggs are added, it becomes smooth. This mixing method contributes to the fudgy texture of the brownies.

5	tablespoons butter
1	ounce unsweetened chocolate
⅔	cup Dutch process or unsweetened cocoa
1½	cups sugar
3	large egg whites, lightly beaten
1	large egg, lightly beaten
1	cup all-purpose flour
½	teaspoon baking powder

Cooking spray

1. Preheat oven to 325°.

2. Melt butter and chocolate in a large saucepan over medium heat. Stir in cocoa; cook 1 minute. Stir in sugar, and cook 1 minute (mixture will almost form a ball and be difficult to stir). Remove pan from heat; cool slightly. Combine egg whites and egg. Gradually add warm chocolate mixture to egg mixture, stirring with a whisk until well blended. Lightly spoon flour into a dry measuring cup, and level with a knife. Combine flour and baking powder; add flour mixture to chocolate mixture, stirring well.

3. Spoon batter into a 9-inch square baking pan coated with cooking spray. Bake at 325° for 27 minutes (do not overbake). Cool in pan on a wire rack. Yield: 20 servings (serving size: 1 brownie).

POINTS value:
3

exchanges:
1½ starch
½ fat

per serving:
Calories 131
Fat 4.3g (saturated fat 1.3g)
Protein 2.5g
Carbohydrate 21.3g
Fiber 0.2g
Cholesterol 11mg
Iron 0.9mg
Sodium 54mg
Calcium 14mg

CHOCOLATE MINT BROWNIES

Chocolate-covered mints melt into the batter of these low-fat brownies.
No one will be able to resist their full-fat flavor.

POINTS value:
3

exchanges:
1½ starch

per serving:
Calories 121
Fat 3.9g (saturated fat 1.1g)
Protein 2.1g
Carbohydrate 19.5g
Fiber 0.2g
Cholesterol 14mg
Iron 0.7mg
Sodium 81mg
Calcium 7mg

Cooking spray
¼ cup butter
32 (about 3 ounces) creamy, small-size mints in pure chocolate (such as Junior Mints)
1 cup all-purpose flour
¼ teaspoon baking soda
⅛ teaspoon salt
⅔ cup sugar
⅓ cup unsweetened cocoa
1 large egg
1 large egg white

1. Preheat oven to 350°.

2. Coat bottom of an 8-inch square baking pan with cooking spray.

3. Place butter and mints in a 2-cup glass measure; microwave at HIGH 30 seconds or until soft. Stir until smooth, and set aside.

4. Lightly spoon flour into a dry measuring cup; level with a knife. Combine flour, baking soda, and salt in a bowl. Combine sugar, cocoa, egg, and egg white in a large bowl; beat with a mixer at medium speed until well blended. Add mint mixture; beat well. Add flour mixture; beat at low speed just until blended. Pour batter into prepared pan. Bake at 350° for 20 to 25 minutes; cool in pan completely on a wire rack. Yield: 16 servings (serving size: 1 brownie).

Note: You can substitute 2 large (1.5-ounce) mints or 6 miniature chocolate-covered peppermint patties (such as York) for 32 Junior Mints.

BUTTERSCOTCH BARS

These bar cookies are an easy option when you need yummy cookies quick and don't have time for rolling, slicing, or dropping dough.

½   cup granulated sugar
½   cup packed brown sugar
¼   cup butter, softened
2   large egg whites
1   teaspoon vanilla extract
1¼ cups all-purpose flour
½   teaspoon baking powder
¼   teaspoon salt
½   cup butterscotch morsels
Cooking spray

1. Preheat oven to 350°.
2. Beat sugars and butter with a mixer at medium speed until well blended (about 4 minutes). Add egg whites and vanilla; beat well. Lightly spoon flour into dry measuring cups, and level with a knife. Combine flour, baking powder, and salt; stir well with a whisk. Add flour mixture to sugar mixture; beat at low speed just until blended. Stir in morsels.
3. Spread batter evenly into an 8-inch square baking pan coated with cooking spray. Bake at 350° for 28 minutes or until a wooden pick inserted in center comes out clean. Cool bars in pan on a wire rack. Yield: 16 servings (serving size: 1 bar).

POINTS value:
3

exchanges:
1½ starch
½ fat

per serving:
Calories 142
Fat 4.3g (saturated fat 2.6g)
Protein 1.6g
Carbohydrate 24g
Fiber 0.3g
Cholesterol 8mg
Iron 0.6mg
Sodium 95mg
Calcium 24mg

MINT-CHOCOLATE TRUFFLES

At your next holiday party, serve these rich chocolate confections in pretty foil petit four cups and arrange them on a cake stand or a lovely tray.

POINTS value:
1

exchanges:
½ starch
½ fat

per serving:
Calories 58
Fat 1.4g (saturated fat 0.8g)
Protein 0.5g
Carbohydrate 11.5g
Fiber 0g
Cholesterol 2mg
Iron 0.1mg
Sodium 10mg
Calcium 3mg

⅓ cup semisweet mint-chocolate morsels
½ cup (4 ounces) block-style ⅓-less-fat cream cheese, softened
1   (16-ounce) package powdered sugar, sifted
¼ cup unsweetened cocoa
¼ cup sifted powdered sugar
2   tablespoons semisweet mint-chocolate morsels

1. Place ⅓ cup morsels in a medium glass bowl, and microwave at HIGH 1 minute or until morsels are almost melted, stirring until smooth. Cool.

2. Add cheese to melted morsels, and beat with a mixer at medium speed until smooth. Add 1 (16-ounce) package powdered sugar to cheese mixture; beat until well blended. Press mixture into a 6-inch square on heavy-duty plastic wrap, and cover with additional plastic wrap. Chill at least 1 hour.

3. Remove top sheet of plastic wrap; cut mixture into 48 squares. Roll each square into a ball, and place on wax paper. Roll half of balls in cocoa; roll remaining balls in ¼ cup powdered sugar.

4. Place 2 tablespoons morsels in a heavy-duty zip-top plastic bag, and microwave at HIGH 30 seconds or until morsels are softened. Knead bag until morsels are smooth. Snip a tiny hole in corner of bag; drizzle chocolate over balls rolled in cocoa. Serve at room temperature. Yield: 48 servings (serving size: 1 truffle).

Note: Store truffles in a single layer in an airtight container in freezer up to 1 month. Let stand at room temperature 1 hour before serving.

Fish
&
Shellfish

prep: 9 minutes ★ cook: 31 minutes ★ other: 20 minutes

GRILLED AMBERJACK WITH CARAMELIZED ONION

While the fish is marinating in the refrigerator, the onion is caramelizing on the grill. If amberjack isn't available, you may substitute mahimahi or swordfish.

POINTS value:
5

exchanges:
½ starch
5 very lean meat

per serving:
Calories 217
Fat 3.2g (saturated fat 1g)
Protein 34g
Carbohydrate 10.6g
Fiber 1g
Cholesterol 66mg
Iron 1.8mg
Sodium 364mg
Calcium 53mg

¼ cup plus 2 tablespoons reduced-calorie maple syrup, divided
3 tablespoons low-sodium teriyaki sauce
1 tablespoon lemon juice
2 teaspoons minced garlic
6 (6-ounce) amberjack fillets
Butter-flavored cooking spray
1 large Vidalia or other sweet onion, thinly sliced
2 teaspoons butter, melted

1. Combine ¼ cup maple syrup, teriyaki sauce, lemon juice, and garlic in a large zip-top plastic bag. Add fish. Seal bag, and shake gently until fish is well coated. Marinate in refrigerator 20 minutes.
2. Prepare grill.
3. While fish marinates, coat 1 side of a 12-inch square of heavy-duty foil with cooking spray. Place onion slices on half of coated side of foil. Combine 2 tablespoons maple syrup and butter, stirring well. Drizzle syrup mixture over onion. Fold foil over onion, and crimp edges to seal.
4. Place foil packet on grill rack. Cover and grill 20 to 25 minutes or until onion is tender and golden. Set aside, and keep warm.
5. Remove fish from marinade, reserving marinade. Place marinade in a small saucepan; bring to a boil, and set aside. Place fish on grill rack coated with cooking spray; cover and grill 4 to 6 minutes on each side or until fish flakes easily when tested with a fork, basting often with reserved marinade. Place fish on a serving platter; top evenly with onion. Yield: 6 servings (serving size: 1 fillet).

CREOLE CATFISH WITH VIDALIA-OLIVE RELISH

*An intriguing blend of spices flavors these catfish fillets,
while the relish—a balance of tangy olives and sweet onions—
provides the perfect finishing touch.*

2   teaspoons olive oil, divided
1   cup chopped Vidalia or other sweet onion
⅓   cup chopped red bell pepper
2   tablespoons chopped pitted green olives
2   tablespoons chopped pitted kalamata olives
2   tablespoons water
1   tablespoon minced fresh thyme, divided
1   tablespoon paprika
¼   teaspoon salt
¼   teaspoon garlic powder
⅛   teaspoon ground red pepper
4   (6-ounce) farm-raised catfish fillets
Cooking spray

1. Heat 1 teaspoon oil in a large nonstick skillet over medium-high heat. Add onion; sauté 5 minutes. Spoon onion into a bowl. Stir in bell pepper, olives, water, and 1 teaspoon thyme. Cover and refrigerate at least 2 hours.
2. Prepare grill.
3. Combine 1 teaspoon oil, 2 teaspoons thyme, paprika, salt, garlic powder, and ground red pepper. Rub paprika mixture over both sides of fish. Place fish on grill rack coated with cooking spray; grill 5 minutes on each side or until fish flakes easily when tested with a fork. Serve with relish. Yield: 4 servings (serving size: 1 fillet and about ⅓ cup relish).

POINTS value:
5

exchanges:
1 vegetable
4 very lean meat
1 fat

per serving:
Calories 211
Fat 9.2g (saturated fat 1.8g)
Protein 25.2g
Carbohydrate 6.6g
Fiber 1.8g
Cholesterol 77mg
Iron 3.5mg
Sodium 308mg
Calcium 93mg

GRILLED GROUPER WITH APRICOT-GINGER RELISH

Grouper can take the heat from the grill and from bold, spicy seasonings like fresh ginger and chile paste with garlic. The sweet apricots tame the "sizzle" in the dish. If you can't find fresh apricots, substitute peaches.

POINTS value:
5

exchanges:
½ starch
5 very lean meat
½ fat

per serving:
Calories 247
Fat 2.5g (saturated fat 0.5g)
Protein 36.8g
Carbohydrate 17.9g
Fiber 2.6g
Cholesterol 67mg
Iron 2.5mg
Sodium 326mg
Calcium 48mg

2   cups diced fresh apricots (about 6 medium)
½   cup diced red bell pepper
⅓   cup rice wine vinegar
¼   cup minced green onions
2   tablespoons sugar
2   tablespoons minced peeled fresh ginger
½   teaspoon freshly ground black pepper
¼   teaspoon salt
¼   teaspoon hot sauce
1   tablespoon chile paste with garlic
4   (6-ounce) grouper fillets (½ inch thick)
Cooking spray

1. Combine first 9 ingredients in a small bowl, and stir well. Cover and let relish stand at room temperature 1 hour.
2. Prepare grill.
3. Rub chile paste over both sides of fish.
4. Place fish on grill rack coated with cooking spray, and grill 6 minutes on each side or until fish flakes easily when tested with a fork. Serve with relish. Yield: 4 servings (serving size: 1 fillet and about ½ cup relish).

OVEN-POACHED HALIBUT PROVENÇALE

pictured on page 78

Poaching is a classic method of cooking that adds flavor but virtually no fat. This recipe uses a moderate oven temperature to accomplish the same results as stovetop poaching. And because poaching preserves the shape and texture of the fish and vegetables, this dish is visually stunning—ideal for entertaining.

Cooking spray
1   cup dry white wine or fat-free, less-sodium chicken broth
6   (6-ounce) halibut steaks
6   cups diced tomato
2   cups finely chopped onion
¼   cup chopped fresh basil
¼   cup chopped fresh parsley
2   tablespoons minced kalamata olives
1   tablespoon olive oil
½   teaspoon salt
½   teaspoon anchovy paste
⅛   teaspoon pepper
2   garlic cloves, minced
¼   cup dry breadcrumbs
1   tablespoon grated Parmesan cheese
1   teaspoon olive oil

POINTS value:
6

exchanges:
½ starch
1 vegetable
5 very lean meat
1 fat

per serving:
Calories 300
Fat 8.6g (saturated fat 1.3g)
Protein 38.8g
Carbohydrate 16.9g
Fiber 3.2g
Cholesterol 81mg
Iron 3mg
Sodium 437mg
Calcium 131mg

1. Preheat oven to 350°.
2. Coat a 13 x 9-inch baking dish with cooking spray. Pour wine into dish, and arrange fish in dish. Combine tomato and next 9 ingredients in a bowl; stir well, and spoon over fish. Bake at 350° for 35 minutes or until fish flakes easily when tested with a fork.
3. Preheat broiler.
4. Combine breadcrumbs, cheese, and 1 teaspoon oil in a bowl. Sprinkle over tomato mixture, and broil until crumbs are golden. Serve immediately with a slotted spatula. Yield: 6 servings (serving size: 1 steak and 1 cup tomato mixture).

GRILLED MAHIMAHI KEBABS WITH PINEAPPLE–MANDARIN SAUCE

Hot, steamed rice is the perfect side dish for these herb-coated fish kebabs that are grilled to perfection and served with a Chinese-inspired sauce.

POINTS value:
8

exchanges:
1 starch
1 fruit
1 vegetable
5 very lean meat
1 fat

per serving:
Calories 392
Fat 7.8g (saturated fat 2g)
Protein 35.1g
Carbohydrate 47.7g
Fiber 2.7g
Cholesterol 66mg
Iron 2.8mg
Sodium 427mg
Calcium 34mg

½ cup chopped onion
⅓ cup honey
½ cup dry red wine or pineapple juice
2 tablespoons balsamic vinegar
2 tablespoons pineapple juice
1 tablespoon low-sodium soy sauce
2 cups diced fresh pineapple
1½ pounds mahimahi steaks, cut into 24 (1-inch) pieces
24 (1-inch) cubes fresh pineapple
24 (1-inch) pieces green bell pepper
1 tablespoon chopped fresh sage
¼ teaspoon salt
¼ teaspoon black pepper
Cooking spray

1. Combine chopped onion and honey in a medium non-stick skillet. Place over medium heat, and cook 12 minutes or until golden brown, stirring occasionally. Add red wine and next 3 ingredients; cook 10 minutes. Stir in diced pineapple, and cook 5 minutes. Keep warm.
2. Prepare grill.
3. Thread 3 mahimahi pieces, 3 pineapple cubes, and 3 bell pepper pieces alternately onto each of 8 (12-inch) skewers. Sprinkle kebabs with sage, salt, and black pepper. Place kebabs on grill rack coated with cooking spray; grill 15 minutes or until fish is done, turning every 5 minutes. Serve with pineapple sauce. Yield: 4 servings (serving size: 2 kebabs and ½ cup pineapple sauce).

CINNAMON-APRICOT GLAZED SALMON

Cinnamon breaks away from the confines of toast and sticky buns
to perk up this top-rated broiled salmon.

2   tablespoons low-sodium soy sauce
1   tablespoon minced peeled fresh ginger
2   (3-inch) cinnamon sticks
1   (12-ounce) can apricot nectar
4   (6-ounce) salmon fillets (about 1 inch thick)

1. Combine first 4 ingredients in a saucepan, and bring to
a boil. Reduce heat, and simmer until reduced to ¾ cup
(about 30 minutes). Strain mixture through a sieve over a
bowl, and discard solids.
2. Preheat broiler.
3. Place fish on a broiler pan lined with foil, and broil 5
minutes. Brush fish with ¼ cup apricot mixture. Broil
3 minutes or until lightly browned and fish flakes easily
when tested with a fork. Serve fish with remaining apricot
mixture. Yield: 4 servings (serving size: 1 fillet and about
2 tablespoons sauce).

Cinnamon: Cinnamon comes from the aromatic bark of a
tree native to Sri Lanka, India, and Burma. Buy it as sticks
(or quills) or ground. Cinnamon sticks have a sweeter, subtler
flavor and a longer shelf life than ground. Cinnamon sticks
are best ground in a clean coffee mill.

POINTS value:
7

exchanges:
½ starch
5 very lean meat

per serving:
Calories 325
Fat 13.1g (saturated fat 3.1g)
Protein 37g
Carbohydrate 13.2g
Fiber 0.6g
Cholesterol 87mg
Iron 1.1mg
Sodium 349mg
Calcium 28mg

GRILLED SALMON WITH GINGER-ORANGE-MUSTARD GLAZE

Putting a delicious meal on the table doesn't get any easier than this! After combining orange juice and a handful of other ingredients, you'll use this mixture as a marinade, a basting glaze, and a sauce to serve with the grilled fish. Just be sure to boil the remaining marinade before serving to kill any bacteria from the raw fish. Serve with cilantro rice.

POINTS value:
8

exchanges:
1 starch
5 lean meat

per serving:
Calories 341
Fat 14.5g (saturated fat 3.1g)
Protein 38.2g
Carbohydrate 13.9g
Fiber 0.4g
Cholesterol 86.8mg
Iron 1.4mg
Sodium 993mg
Calcium 47mg

¼ cup fresh orange juice
¼ cup low-sodium soy sauce
¼ cup cream sherry or orange juice
¼ cup Dijon mustard
2 tablespoons grated peeled fresh ginger
2 tablespoons honey
4 (6-ounce) salmon fillets (about 1 inch thick)
Cooking spray

1. Combine first 6 ingredients in a large zip-top plastic bag. Add fish to bag; seal and marinate in refrigerator 30 minutes. Remove fish from bag, reserving marinade.
2. Prepare grill or broiler.
3. Place fish on grill rack or broiler pan coated with cooking spray. Cook 5 minutes on each side or until fish flakes easily when tested with a fork, basting frequently with reserved marinade.
4. Place remaining marinade in a saucepan; bring to a boil. Serve with fish. Yield: 4 servings (serving size: 1 fillet and 3 tablespoons glaze).

Getting to Know Sherry: Sherry is a fortified non-vintage wine that ranges in color, flavor, sweetness, and quality. Traditionally from Spain, sherry is now produced in other countries such as the United States, Australia, and South Africa.

STEAMED SEA BASS ON SPINACH WITH LEMON SAUCE

1	lemon
1	lime
¼	cup minced shallots
2	teaspoons butter
2	teaspoons olive oil
½	teaspoon salt, divided
2	teaspoons chopped fresh dill
4	(6-ounce) sea bass or other firm white fish fillets (about 1½ inches thick)
¼	teaspoon pepper, divided
2	cups water
1	(10-ounce) package fresh spinach, trimmed

1. Peel and section lemon and lime over a large bowl; squeeze membranes to extract juice, reserving 3 tablespoons juice. Set lemon and lime sections aside; discard membranes and rind.
2. Combine sections, reserved 3 tablespoons juice, shallots, butter, oil, and ⅛ teaspoon salt in a small saucepan; bring to a boil. Remove from heat; stir in dill.
3. Sprinkle fish with ¼ teaspoon salt and ⅛ teaspoon pepper. Arrange fish in a steamer basket. Place 2 cups water in a Dutch oven; place steamer basket in pan, and bring to a boil. Steam fish, covered, 12 minutes or until fish flakes easily when tested with a fork.
4. Place spinach in a large nonstick skillet over medium-high heat; sauté 3 minutes or until wilted. Sprinkle spinach with ⅛ teaspoon salt and ⅛ teaspoon pepper. Place ½ cup spinach on each of 4 plates; top each portion with 1 fillet and about 3 tablespoons lemon sauce. Yield: 4 servings.

POINTS **value:**
5

exchanges:
1 vegetable
5 very lean meat
1 fat

per serving:
Calories 246
Fat 8g (saturated fat 2.4g)
Protein 34.5g
Carbohydrate 11.7g
Fiber 3.6g
Cholesterol 75mg
Iron 3.1mg
Sodium 489mg
Calcium 124mg

MALAYSIAN LIME-COCONUT SWORDFISH
pictured on page 77

Lemon grass imparts a characteristic citrus flavor and fragrance to many Asian dishes. You'll find this herb with long, thin, gray-green leaves in the produce section of many supermarkets. You can substitute grated lemon peel, but cut the amount by half. Serve the swordfish with hot, cooked somen or other Asian noodles.

POINTS value:
6

exchanges:
1 vegetable
4 lean meat

per serving:
Calories 255
Fat 8.5g (saturated fat 2.7g)
Protein 36.8g
Carbohydrate 5.4g
Fiber 0.2g
Cholesterol 71mg
Iron 2mg
Sodium 840mg
Calcium 18mg

⅓ cup light coconut milk
¼ cup chopped fresh cilantro
1 tablespoon brown sugar
2 tablespoons thinly sliced peeled fresh lemon grass (about 1 stalk) or 1 tablespoon grated lemon rind
2 tablespoons fish sauce
1 teaspoon fresh lime juice
½ teaspoon Thai chile paste (such as Dynasty)
2 shallots, peeled and halved
1 garlic clove, peeled and halved
1 (1½-pound) swordfish steak (about 1 inch thick)
Cooking spray
Cilantro sprigs (optional)
Lemon wedges (optional)

1. Preheat broiler.
2. Place first 9 ingredients in a food processor; pulse 3 times or until coarsely chopped. Place fish on a broiler pan coated with cooking spray; spread ½ cup shallot mixture evenly over fish. Broil 15 minutes or until fish flakes easily when tested with a fork. Serve fish with remaining shallot mixture, and garnish with cilantro sprigs and lemon wedges, if desired. Yield: 4 servings (serving size: 5 ounces fish and 2 tablespoons sauce).

TERIYAKI TUNA WITH FRESH PINEAPPLE

Tangy teriyaki and sweet pineapple combine in a marinade for hearty tuna.
Be sure to remove the tuna from the marinade after 30 minutes; otherwise, the
acid will begin to "cook" the fish.

1	small pineapple, peeled and cored
¼	cup low-sodium soy sauce
3	tablespoons honey
3	tablespoons mirin (sweet rice wine) or pineapple juice
2	teaspoons minced peeled fresh ginger
½	teaspoon hot sauce
1	garlic clove, minced
6	(6-ounce) tuna steaks (about ¾ inch thick)

Cooking spray

1. Cut pineapple lengthwise into 6 spears. Combine soy sauce and next 5 ingredients in a large zip-top plastic bag. Add pineapple spears and fish to bag; seal and marinate in refrigerator 30 minutes, turning once. Remove fish and pineapple from bag, reserving marinade.
2. Prepare grill.
3. Place fish and pineapple on grill rack coated with cooking spray; grill 4 minutes on each side or until fish is medium-rare or desired degree of doneness, basting fish frequently with reserved marinade. Discard remaining marinade. Yield: 6 servings (serving size: 1 steak and 1 pineapple spear).

POINTS value:
7

exchanges:
½ starch
½ fruit
4 lean meat

per serving:
Calories 326
Fat 9.1g (saturated fat 2.2g)
Protein 40.3g
Carbohydrate 20.7g
Fiber 1.8g
Cholesterol 65mg
Iron 2.4mg
Sodium 149mg
Calcium 11mg

MUSSELS MARINARA
pictured on page 114

An all-around winner, this recipe presents mussels infused with garlic, parsley, and tomatoes on a bed of pasta for an impressive dinner-party entrée.

POINTS value:
7

exchanges:
3 starch
3 very lean meat
1 fat

per serving:
Calories 369
Fat 8.2g (saturated fat 1.4g)
Protein 30g
Carbohydrate 44.5g
Fiber 4g
Cholesterol 56mg
Iron 10.6mg
Sodium 833mg
Calcium 105mg

5	ounces uncooked linguine
1	tablespoon olive oil
2	cups finely chopped onion
6	garlic cloves, minced
4	cups chopped tomato
1	cup dry white wine or fat-free, less-sodium chicken broth
⅔	cup chopped fresh flat-leaf parsley
¼	cup chopped fresh basil
½	teaspoon salt
1	teaspoon black pepper
½	teaspoon crushed red pepper
2	bay leaves
4½	pounds fresh mussels (about 100 mussels), scrubbed and debearded

Basil sprigs (optional)

1. Cook pasta according to package directions, omitting salt and fat.

2. While pasta cooks, heat oil in a large stockpot over medium-high heat. Add onion and garlic; sauté 3 minutes. Add tomato and next 7 ingredients; cook over medium heat 10 minutes. Add mussels; cover and cook 10 minutes or until shells open. Discard bay leaves and any unopened shells. Place pasta in wide, shallow bowls. Remove mussels with a slotted spoon, and place over pasta. Spoon tomato mixture over mussels. Garnish with basil sprigs, if desired. Yield: 5 servings (serving size: about 20 mussels, ½ cup pasta, and 1 cup tomato mixture).

PARMESAN SCALLOPS WITH SPINACH ALFREDO

pictured on page 79

1   (1.6-ounce) package alfredo sauce mix (such as Knorr)
2   cups fat-free milk
Cooking spray
3   cups sliced fresh mushrooms
1   (10-ounce) package fresh spinach, trimmed
¾   cup grated Parmesan cheese
¾   teaspoon dried Italian seasoning
1½   pounds sea scallops

1. Prepare sauce mix according to package directions using 2 cups fat-free milk. Keep warm.
2. Coat a Dutch oven with cooking spray; place over medium-high heat until hot. Add mushrooms; sauté 5 minutes or until tender. Reduce heat to medium. Add spinach, and sauté just until spinach wilts. Remove from heat; stir in alfredo sauce.
3. Combine Parmesan cheese and Italian seasoning in a pie plate or shallow dish; stir well. Dredge scallops in cheese mixture. Place a large nonstick skillet over medium-high heat until hot. Coat 1 side of half of scallops with cooking spray. Add scallops to pan, cooking spray side down; cook 3 minutes or until golden. Coat top of scallops with cooking spray; turn scallops over, and cook 2 minutes or until done. Remove scallops from pan; set aside, and keep warm. Repeat procedure with remaining half of scallops.
4. Spoon spinach mixture into shallow bowls, and top with scallops. Yield: 4 servings (serving size: about 4 ounces scallops and about ¾ cup spinach alfredo).

POINTS value:
7

exchanges:
1 starch
1 vegetable
5 lean meat

per serving:
Calories 356
Fat 9.4g (saturated fat 5g)
Protein 46.1g
Carbohydrate 21g
Fiber 2.6g
Cholesterol 77mg
Iron 3.2mg
Sodium 1,298mg
Calcium 526mg

SHRIMP KEBABS WITH JALAPEÑO–LIME MARINADE
pictured on page 2

You'll appreciate the versatility of this recipe. You can substitute 1½ pounds pork tenderloin or skinless, boneless chicken breast, cut into 1-inch cubes, for the shrimp. In fact, try all three—you'll love the results. If the weather is pretty, fire up the grill. When the weather doesn't permit, the broiler works just as well.

POINTS value:
4

exchanges:
1 starch
1 vegetable
3 very lean meat

per serving:
Calories 217
Fat 2.4g (saturated fat 0.4g)
Protein 24.2g
Carbohydrate 25.1g
Fiber 0.7g
Cholesterol 172mg
Iron 3.7mg
Sodium 269mg
Calcium 80mg

2 pounds large shrimp, peeled, deveined, and butterflied
½ cup thawed orange juice concentrate, undiluted
1 teaspoon grated lime rind
¼ cup fresh lime juice
¼ cup honey
2 teaspoons ground cumin
¼ teaspoon salt
3 garlic cloves, minced
2 jalapeño peppers, seeded and chopped
2 red bell peppers, cut into 1-inch cubes
Lime wedges (optional)
Cooking spray

1. Combine first 9 ingredients in a large zip-top plastic bag; seal and marinate in refrigerator 30 minutes. Remove shrimp from bag, reserving marinade. Thread shrimp, bell pepper cubes, and, if desired, lime wedges onto each of 6 skewers.
2. Prepare grill or broiler.
3. Place kebabs on grill rack or broiler pan coated with cooking spray; cook 4 minutes on each side or until shrimp are done, basting frequently with marinade. Discard remaining marinade. Yield: 6 servings (serving size: 1 kebab).

Malaysian Lime-Coconut Swordfish, page 72

Oven-Poached Halibut Provençale,
page 67

Parmesan Scallops with Spinach Alfredo, page 75

Spanish Sherried Shrimp

SPANISH SHERRIED SHRIMP

pictured on facing page

You can't bring the entire Mediterranean home, but with this easy adaptation of a Spanish classic, everyone will think you did. Serve with long-grain rice tossed with garlic and toasted slivered almonds.

1	tablespoon all-purpose flour
2¼	teaspoons chopped fresh thyme
½	teaspoon salt, divided
¼	teaspoon black pepper
1	pound medium shrimp, peeled and deveined
1	tablespoon olive oil
1½	cups chopped onion
1½	cups chopped red or green bell pepper
3	garlic cloves, minced
⅓	cup medium dry sherry or fat-free, less-sodium chicken broth
1	(14.5-ounce) can no-salt-added whole tomatoes, undrained and chopped
2	teaspoons sherry vinegar or white wine vinegar

POINTS value:
4

exchanges:
2 vegetable
3 very lean meat
1 fat

per serving:
Calories 196
Fat 5.3g (saturated fat 0.8g)
Protein 19.7g
Carbohydrate 17.2g
Fiber 2.2g
Cholesterol 129mg
Iron 3.9mg
Sodium 453mg
Calcium 106mg

1. Combine flour, thyme, ¼ teaspoon salt, and black pepper in a large zip-top plastic bag. Add shrimp; seal and shake well.

2. Heat oil in a large nonstick skillet over medium-high heat. Add shrimp, and sauté 3 minutes. Remove shrimp from pan; set aside. Add onion, bell pepper, and garlic; sauté 2 minutes. Add sherry; cook 1 minute. Add ¼ teaspoon salt and tomatoes; cook 4 minutes. Stir in shrimp and vinegar. Yield: 4 servings (serving size: 1½ cups).

GARLIC-LOVER'S SHRIMP

For a truly memorable meal, offer these shrimp, bathed in a garlic-wine sauce, with a salad and some crusty bread to dip in the sauce.

POINTS value:
4

exchanges:
4 very lean meat
½ fat

per serving:
Calories 177
Fat 5.6g (saturated fat 0.9g)
Protein 26.4g
Carbohydrate 3.8g
Fiber 0.2g
Cholesterol 194mg
Iron 3.5mg
Sodium 340mg
Calcium 84mg

1	tablespoon olive oil
¼	teaspoon crushed red pepper
8	garlic cloves, minced
1	bay leaf
1½	pounds large shrimp, peeled and deveined
¼	teaspoon salt
½	cup dry white wine or fat-free, less-sodium chicken broth
2	tablespoons minced fresh parsley
¾	teaspoon minced fresh thyme

1. Heat oil in a large nonstick skillet over medium-high heat. Add pepper, garlic, and bay leaf; sauté 30 seconds. Add shrimp and salt; sauté 3 minutes. Remove shrimp from pan; set aside. Add wine, parsley, and thyme; bring to a boil, and cook until reduced to ¼ cup (about 1 minute). Return shrimp to pan; toss to coat. Discard bay leaf. Yield: 4 servings (serving size: about 1 cup).

How Much to Buy?
To save prep time, instead of peeling and deveining your own shrimp, you can buy peeled and deveined raw shrimp at the seafood counter of most supermarkets. If your recipe calls for unpeeled raw shrimp, use the chart below to determine the amount of peeled and deveined shrimp to buy.

Unpeeled Raw Shrimp		Peeled and Deveined Raw Shrimp
⅔ pound	=	½ pound
1 pound	=	¾ pound
1⅓ pounds	=	1 pound
2 pounds	=	1½ pounds
2⅔ pounds	=	2 pounds
4 pounds	=	3 pounds

Meatless
Main Dishes

ROASTED BELL PEPPER AND OLIVE PIZZAS

Invite friends over for an informal dinner and let them help make these crowd-pleasing pizzas. It's a simple way to get everyone involved, inspire conversation, and entertain with ease. To feed a smaller group, cut all the ingredients by half and make one pizza.

POINTS value:
5

exchanges:
2 starch
1 fat

per serving:
Calories 215
Fat 5.6g (saturated fat 1.9g)
Protein 9g
Carbohydrate 32.1g
Fiber 1.1g
Cholesterol 3.1mg
Iron 2.3mg
Sodium 467mg
Calcium 226mg

2 large red bell peppers
2 large yellow bell peppers
½ cup sliced green olives
¼ cup chopped fresh parsley
2 teaspoons capers
2 teaspoons red wine vinegar
1 teaspoon olive oil
⅛ teaspoon black pepper
2 (14-ounce) Italian cheese-flavored pizza crusts (such as Boboli)
6 tablespoons grated fresh Parmesan cheese

1. Preheat broiler.

2. Cut bell peppers in half lengthwise; discard seeds and membranes. Place bell pepper halves, skin sides up, on a foil-lined baking sheet, and flatten with hand. Broil 15 minutes or until blackened. Place in a zip-top plastic bag, and seal. Let stand 15 minutes. Peel peppers, and cut into strips. Combine bell pepper strips, green olives, and next 5 ingredients in a bowl.

3. Preheat oven to 450°.

4. Place pizza crusts on baking sheets. Divide bell pepper mixture evenly between pizza crusts; sprinkle evenly with cheese. Bake at 450° for 8 to 10 minutes or until cheese melts. Remove pizzas to a cutting board. Cut each pizza into 6 wedges. Yield: 12 servings (serving size: 1 wedge).

Note: Instead of roasting your own peppers, you may substitute bottled roasted red bell peppers. You will need to cut enough of the bottled peppers into strips to measure about 1⅓ cups.

FRESH TOMATO, BASIL, AND CHEESE PIZZA
pictured on page 1

It takes only a few ingredients to create a fabulous pizza when you use the best summer has to offer—vine-ripened tomatoes, garden-fresh basil, and garlic. Pair them with a store-bought crust, and dinner is done in less than 30 minutes.

1 (14-ounce) Italian cheese-flavored pizza crust (such as Boboli)
2 teaspoons olive oil
½ cup (2 ounces) grated fresh Parmesan cheese, divided
3 tomatoes (about 1½ pounds), cut into ¼-inch slices
6 garlic cloves, thinly sliced
¼ teaspoon salt
⅛ teaspoon pepper
¼ cup fresh basil leaves

POINTS value:
5

exchanges:
2 starch
1 vegetable
½ high-fat meat
1 fat

per serving:
Calories 256
Fat 8g (saturated fat 3.1g)
Protein 11.8g
Carbohydrate 34.5g
Fiber 2g
Cholesterol 7mg
Iron 2.4mg
Sodium 617mg
Calcium 306mg

1. Preheat oven to 450°.
2. Place pizza crust on a baking sheet. Brush crust with olive oil. Sprinkle with ¼ cup Parmesan cheese, leaving a ½-inch border around edge of crust. Arrange tomato slices over cheese, overlapping edges; top with garlic slices, ¼ cup cheese, salt, and pepper.
3. Bake at 450° for 8 to 10 minutes or until crust is golden. Remove pizza to a cutting board, and top with fresh basil leaves. Let stand 5 minutes. Cut into 12 squares. Yield: 6 servings (serving size: 2 squares).

Basil Basics: Basil is one of the most important culinary herbs. Sweet basil, the most common type, smells of licorice and cloves. It's readily available year-round in the produce section of the supermarket. Used in sauces, sandwiches, soups, and salads, basil is in top form when married to tomatoes.

FRITTATA WITH SWISS CHARD, POTATOES, AND FONTINA

Swiss chard, a beautiful, often overlooked vegetable, is at its best in spring. It tastes like a combination of spinach and beets (its cousins), but has a meatier texture. Use both the leaves and stems after cleaning them thoroughly.

POINTS value:
6

exchanges:
1½ starch
1 vegetable
½ high-fat meat
1 fat

per serving:
Calories 257
Fat 10.2g (saturated fat 4.9g)
Protein 15.7g
Carbohydrate 26.2g
Fiber 2.2g
Cholesterol 186mg
Iron 3.1mg
Sodium 565mg
Calcium 172mg

6   cups coarsely chopped Swiss chard (about 8 ounces)
⅓   cup water
2   cups diced baking potato (about ¾ pound)
½   teaspoon salt, divided
⅓   cup fat-free milk
¼   cup chopped fresh parsley
¼   teaspoon pepper
4   large egg whites
3   large eggs
1½ teaspoons butter
Cooking spray
½   cup (2 ounces) shredded fontina or Swiss cheese

1. Combine Swiss chard and water in a large saucepan over medium heat. Cover and cook 10 minutes or until Swiss chard is tender. Drain and cool.
2. While Swiss chard cooks, place potato in a saucepan; cover with water. Bring to a boil; cook 8 minutes or until tender. Drain and cool. Toss potato with ¼ teaspoon salt. Set aside.
3. Combine ¼ teaspoon salt, milk, and next 4 ingredients in a large bowl; stir with a whisk. Stir in potato and Swiss chard. Melt butter in a medium nonstick skillet coated with cooking spray over medium heat. Pour egg mixture into pan. Cover, reduce heat, and cook 10 minutes until almost set. Sprinkle with cheese.
4. Preheat broiler.
5. Wrap handle of skillet with foil. Broil 5 minutes or until golden brown. Yield: 4 servings (serving size: 1 wedge).

SPINACH, RICE, AND FETA PIE

Eating healthfully just got easier with this innovative, hearty spinach pie. Complete the meal with a serving of sliced strawberries or blueberries.

2 teaspoons butter
¾ cup chopped onion
2 teaspoons all-purpose flour
½ teaspoon salt
¼ teaspoon pepper
1½ cups 1% low-fat milk
2 cups cooked long-grain rice
¾ cup (3 ounces) crumbled feta cheese
1 large egg, lightly beaten
2 large egg whites, lightly beaten
1 (10-ounce) package frozen chopped spinach, thawed, drained, and squeezed dry
Olive oil-flavored cooking spray
2 tablespoons grated fresh Parmesan cheese

POINTS value:
4

exchanges:
1½ starch
1 vegetable
½ high-fat meat
½ fat

per serving:
Calories 212
Fat 8g (saturated fat 4.3g)
Protein 10.8g
Carbohydrate 24.5g
Fiber 2.1g
Cholesterol 57mg
Iron 2mg
Sodium 565mg
Calcium 268mg

1. Preheat oven to 400°.

2. Melt butter in a large saucepan over medium heat. Add onion, and sauté 3 minutes. Stir in flour, salt, and pepper. Gradually add milk, stirring with a whisk until well blended. Bring mixture to a simmer, and cook 1 minute or until slightly thick, stirring constantly. Remove saucepan from heat, and stir in cooked rice, crumbled feta cheese, egg, egg whites, and spinach.

3. Pour mixture into a 9-inch pie plate coated with cooking spray. Sprinkle Parmesan cheese over pie. Bake at 400° for 35 minutes or until set. Yield: 6 servings (serving size: 1 wedge).

POTATO AND CHEESE PATTIES

The vibrant taste and golden, crisp crust on these patties made them a big hit in our Test Kitchens. Serve with a tossed salad for a filling meatless meal.

POINTS value:
7

exchanges:
3 starch
1 vegetable
2 fat

per serving:
Calories 345
Fat 10.9g (saturated fat 3.3g)
Protein 10g
Carbohydrate 53.3g
Fiber 4.2g
Cholesterol 14mg
Iron 1.3mg
Sodium 776mg
Calcium 146mg

1 teaspoon kosher salt, divided
2 medium baking potatoes (about 1¼ pounds), peeled and quartered
¾ cup (3 ounces) crumbled queso fresco or shredded Monterey Jack cheese
2 tablespoons minced green onions
¼ teaspoon freshly ground black pepper
1 tablespoon olive oil
6 tablespoons diced tomato
¼ cup julienne-cut red onion

1. Place ½ teaspoon salt and potatoes in a saucepan, and cover with water. Bring to a boil; reduce heat, and simmer 15 minutes or until tender. Drain, and mash with a potato masher until smooth. Cool.

2. Add cheese, green onions, ½ teaspoon salt, and pepper to potato mixture, stirring well. Divide potato mixture into 6 balls (about ½ cup per ball). Flatten balls into ½-inch-thick patties (about 3-inch diameter). Place on a baking sheet; cover and refrigerate 20 minutes or until firm.

3. Heat oil in a large nonstick skillet over medium heat. Place patties in pan; cook 5 minutes or until bottoms are browned. Turn patties; cook 3 minutes. Top patties with diced tomato and red onion. Yield: 2 servings (serving size: 3 patties, 3 tablespoons tomato, and about 2 tablespoons onion).

STUFFED POBLANOS

1   (8-ounce) package black beans and rice mix
10 large poblano chiles
1   cup frozen whole-kernel corn, thawed
1   cup (4 ounces) shredded reduced-fat Monterey Jack
    cheese
1   (15-ounce) can no-salt-added crushed tomatoes,
    undrained
1   (15½-ounce) jar mild salsa

1. Preheat oven to 350°.
2. Cook rice mix according to package directions, omitting fat.
3. While rice mix cooks, cut a lengthwise strip from each chile. Chop enough of chile strips to measure ½ cup; reserve remaining strips for another use. Remove and discard seeds from chiles. Cook chile halves in boiling water 5 minutes; drain and set aside.
4. Combine rice mix, chopped chile, corn, cheese, and tomatoes. Spoon evenly into chile halves; place chiles in a 13 x 9-inch baking dish. Add hot water to dish to a depth of ¼ inch. Bake at 350° for 20 minutes or until thoroughly heated.
5. Place salsa in a food processor; process until smooth. Spoon salsa onto plates, and top with stuffed chiles. Yield: 5 servings (serving size: 2 stuffed chiles and about ⅓ cup salsa).

POINTS value:
7

exchanges:
3 starch
2 vegetable
1 medium-fat meat

per serving:
Calories 344
Fat 7.3g (saturated fat 3.4g)
Protein 16.7g
Carbohydrate 59.8g
Fiber 7g
Cholesterol 18mg
Iron 5mg
Sodium 1,355mg
Calcium 247mg

Chile Prep

Cut a strip from the long side of each chile.

Chop enough of the chile strips to get ½ cup.

Meatless Main Dishes **89**

prep: 8 minutes ★ **cook:** 12 minutes ★ **other:** 5 minutes

SPAGHETTI SQUASH WITH WHITE BEAN PROVENÇALE

When scraped out with the tines of a fork, the cooked flesh of the squash resembles spaghetti. Garlic, tomatoes, and olive oil complement spaghetti squash. If you can't find roasted garlic-flavored oil, use regular vegetable oil and ½ teaspoon minced garlic.

POINTS value:
4

exchanges:
2 starch
2 vegetable

per serving:
Calories 226
Fat 2.9g (saturated fat 0.6g)
Protein 10.5g
Carbohydrate 43g
Fiber 6.8g
Cholesterol 0mg
Iron 6.9mg
Sodium 508mg
Calcium 115mg

1 (2½-pound) spaghetti squash
Cooking spray
1 teaspoon roasted garlic-flavored vegetable oil
2 cups thinly sliced leek (about 1 leek)
2 (16-ounce) cans navy beans, rinsed and drained
1 (14½-ounce) can no-salt–added stewed tomatoes, undrained
2 tablespoons chopped ripe olives
1 tablespoon balsamic vinegar
¼ teaspoon salt
¼ teaspoon pepper

1. Pierce squash 6 to 8 times with a fork. Place squash on a layer of paper towels in microwave oven. Microwave, uncovered, at HIGH 12 to 15 minutes or until squash is soft to the touch, turning squash over every 5 minutes. Let stand 5 minutes. Cut squash in half lengthwise; remove and discard seeds. Using a fork, remove 3 cups spaghetti-like strands from squash; place on a platter, set aside, and keep warm. Reserve any remaining squash for another use.
2. While squash cooks, coat a saucepan with cooking spray; add oil. Place over medium-high heat until hot. Add leek; sauté 3 minutes or until tender. Add beans and tomato; cook over medium heat 5 minutes. Stir in olives and next 3 ingredients; cook until thoroughly heated. Spoon bean mixture over squash. Yield: 4 servings (serving size: about ¾ cup spaghetti squash and about 1⅓ cups bean mixture).

prep: 23 minutes ★ **cook:** 25 minutes

POLENTA WITH ROASTED VEGETABLES

Carefully turn the polenta slices with a spatula—they're soft on the bottom after the first side has been broiled.

4 cups (1-inch) pieces zucchini (about 2 large)
2½ cups (1-inch) pieces red bell pepper (about 2 peppers)
1 cup (1-inch) pieces red onion
1 tablespoon olive oil
Cooking spray
⅓ cup chopped fresh basil
1½ tablespoons balsamic vinegar
¼ teaspoon black pepper, divided
1 (16-ounce) tube refrigerated prepared polenta, cut crosswise into 12 slices
¼ teaspoon salt
¾ cup (3 ounces) crumbled goat or feta cheese

1. Preheat oven to 475°.
2. Combine first 4 ingredients in a large bowl; toss gently to coat. Arrange vegetables in a single layer on a jelly-roll pan coated with cooking spray. Bake at 475° for 25 minutes or until tender, stirring after 15 minutes. Stir in chopped basil, vinegar, and ⅛ teaspoon black pepper.
3. While vegetables roast, sprinkle both sides of polenta slices with ⅛ teaspoon black pepper and salt; coat with cooking spray. Place a large nonstick skillet over medium-high heat. Add polenta slices; cook 4 minutes on each side or until browned. Serve roasted vegetables over polenta; sprinkle with cheese. Yield: 4 servings (serving size: ¾ cup vegetables, 3 polenta slices, and 3 tablespoons cheese).

POINTS value:
6

exchanges:
1½ starch
2 vegetable
1 low-fat meat
1 fat

per serving:
Calories 267
Fat 11.6g (saturated fat 5.8g)
Protein 11.2g
Carbohydrate 29.9g
Fiber 3.8g
Cholesterol 22mg
Iron 2.2mg
Sodium 435mg
Calcium 228mg

RAPID RISOTTO

A pressure cooker is the must-have tool that saves you preparation time and lots of stir-ring. If you're not going meatless tonight, stir in ¾ cup (3 ounces) chopped prosciutto for a real treat. With prosciutto, a 1-cup serving has a **POINTS** value of 6.

POINTS value:
6

exchanges:
3 starch
1 fat

per serving:
Calories 297
Fat 8.2g (saturated fat 3.1g)
Protein 10.2g
Carbohydrate 45.9g
Fiber 2.4g
Cholesterol 10mg
Iron 3mg
Sodium 670mg
Calcium 198mg

1   tablespoon olive oil
1   cup uncooked Arborio rice or other short-grain rice
½   cup frozen chopped onion
½   cup dry white wine or vegetable broth
1   (14-ounce) can vegetable broth (such as Swanson)
1   cup finely chopped plum tomatoes (about ¼ pound)
2   tablespoons chopped fresh parsley
½   teaspoon freshly ground pepper
½   cup (2 ounces) preshredded fresh Parmesan cheese

1. Heat oil in a 6-quart pressure cooker over medium heat until hot. Add rice and onion, and sauté 1 minute. Stir in wine and broth. Close lid securely, and bring to high pressure over high heat (about 4 minutes). Adjust heat to medium or level needed to maintain high pressure, and cook 3 minutes. Remove from heat, and let stand 5 minutes. Place pressure cooker under cold running water. Remove lid, and stir in tomatoes, parsley, and pepper. Cook, uncovered, over medium-high heat 3 minutes, stirring constantly. Stir in cheese. Yield: 4 servings (serving size: 1 cup).

ORZO AND PORTOBELLO CASSEROLE

Savor every delicious bite of this pasta casserole. A variety of sautéed veggies contributes bold flavors to the orzo as it simmers under a layer of bubbly cheese.

¼	cup chopped sun-dried tomatoes, packed without oil
¼	cup boiling water
2	cups uncooked orzo (rice-shaped pasta)
1	tablespoon olive oil
2	cups sliced leek (about 2)
2	cups thinly sliced fennel bulb (about 1 large)
2	cups diced portobello mushroom caps
1	cup mushrooms, quartered
2	garlic cloves, minced
1	cup tomato juice
2	tablespoons minced fresh basil
2	tablespoons balsamic vinegar
1	teaspoon paprika
¼	teaspoon salt
⅛	teaspoon pepper
1	cup (4 ounces) shredded sharp provolone cheese
¼	cup (1 ounce) grated fresh Parmesan cheese

***POINTS* value:**
7

exchanges:
2½ starch
2 vegetable
½ high-fat meat
1 fat

per serving:
Calories 330
Fat 9.4g (saturated fat 4.2g)
Protein 15.1g
Carbohydrate 47.8g
Fiber 3g
Cholesterol 15mg
Iron 4.6mg
Sodium 576mg
Calcium 252mg

1. Combine tomatoes and boiling water in a small bowl; cover and let stand 10 minutes or until tomatoes are soft. Drain tomatoes.

2. While tomatoes stand, cook pasta according to package directions, omitting salt and fat.

3. Heat oil in a large Dutch oven over medium-high heat. Add tomatoes, leek, fennel, mushrooms, and garlic; sauté 15 minutes or until vegetables are tender, stirring occasionally. Stir in orzo. Combine tomato juice and next 5 ingredients in a small bowl.

4. Pour juice mixture over orzo mixture. Cover, reduce heat to medium, and simmer 10 minutes or until liquid is almost absorbed, stirring occasionally. Sprinkle cheeses over orzo mixture; cover and cook 10 minutes or until cheese melts. Yield: 6 servings (serving size: 1⅔ cups).

ROASTED VEGETABLE MACARONI AND CHEESE

POINTS value:
5

exchanges:
1½ starch
2 vegetable
1 high-fat meat

per serving:
Calories 273
Fat 7.1g (saturated fat 3.6g)
Protein 13.7g
Carbohydrate 39g
Fiber 2.8g
Cholesterol 14.7mg
Iron 2.1mg
Sodium 317mg
Calcium 273mg

3 cups diced peeled eggplant (about ¾ pound)
2 cups sliced mushrooms
1 cup coarsely chopped red bell pepper
1 cup coarsely chopped yellow bell pepper
1 cup coarsely chopped onion
1 small zucchini, quartered lengthwise and sliced
2 teaspoons olive oil
4 garlic cloves, minced
12 ounces uncooked medium elbow macaroni
½ cup all-purpose flour
2¾ cups 1% low-fat milk
¾ cup (3 ounces) shredded sharp provolone cheese
¾ cup (3 ounces) grated fresh Parmesan cheese, divided
¼ teaspoon salt
¼ teaspoon freshly ground black pepper
Cooking spray
⅛ teaspoon paprika

1. Preheat oven to 450°.

2. Combine first 8 ingredients in a large shallow roasting pan; toss well. Bake at 450° for 30 minutes or until lightly browned, stirring occasionally. Remove from oven; set aside. Reduce oven temperature to 375°.

3. While vegetables roast, cook macaroni according to package directions, omitting salt and fat.

4. While vegetables and macaroni cook, lightly spoon flour into a dry measuring cup; level with a knife. Combine flour and milk in a large saucepan, stirring with a whisk until blended. Cook over medium heat 8 minutes or until thick, stirring constantly. Add provolone cheese, ½ cup Parmesan cheese, salt, and pepper; cook 3 minutes, stirring frequently. Stir in roasted vegetables and macaroni.

5. Spoon into a 3-quart casserole coated with cooking spray. Combine remaining ¼ cup Parmesan cheese and paprika; sprinkle over mixture. Bake at 375° for 20 minutes or until bubbly. Yield: 10 servings (serving size: 1 cup).

RIGATONI WITH GOAT CHEESE, SUN-DRIED TOMATOES, AND KALE

Creamy goat cheese contributes a delightful tang as it melts around the warm pasta.

½   cup sun-dried tomato sprinkles
2   cups boiling water
12   ounces uncooked rigatoni
½   teaspoon chili oil or vegetable oil
¼   cup minced shallots or minced green onions
6   garlic cloves, minced
4   cups coarsely chopped kale
1½ teaspoons minced fresh oregano
⅛   teaspoon salt
⅛   teaspoon freshly ground pepper
½   cup (2 ounces) crumbled goat cheese

POINTS value:
8

exchanges:
4 starch
2 vegetable
1 fat

per serving:
Calories 396
Fat 5.8g (saturated fat 2.7g)
Protein 15.7g
Carbohydrate 72.3g
Fiber 4.4g
Cholesterol 13mg
Iron 4.4mg
Sodium 484mg
Calcium 200mg

1. Combine tomato sprinkles and boiling water in a bowl; let stand 30 minutes. Drain tomatoes in a sieve over a bowl, reserving ½ cup liquid.
2. While tomatoes stand, cook pasta according to package directions, omitting salt and fat.
3. Heat oil in a large nonstick skillet over medium-high heat. Add shallots and garlic; sauté 1 minute. Add kale; sauté 3 minutes or until wilted. Add tomatoes; sauté 2 minutes. Add reserved ½ cup liquid, oregano, salt, and pepper. Reduce heat; simmer 3 minutes or until kale is tender.
4. Combine pasta, kale mixture, and goat cheese in a large bowl, and toss well. Yield: 4 servings (serving size: 1½ cups).

Note: Substitute 1 cup thawed frozen chopped kale for fresh, if desired.

PASTA PUTTANESCA
pictured on page 115

When you want to jazz up spaghetti night, try this zesty Italian classic. With tomatoes, olives, and anchovy paste, it's sure to be a hit with the entire family.

POINTS value:
6

exchanges:
3 starch
1 vegetable
1 fat

per serving:
Calories 300
Fat 6.6g (saturated fat 0.9g)
Protein 9.7g
Carbohydrate 51.6g
Fiber 3.6g
Cholesterol 0mg
Iron 3.7mg
Sodium 696mg
Calcium 47mg

8   ounces uncooked vermicelli
1   tablespoon olive oil
3   garlic cloves, minced
3½ cups diced plum tomato (about 1 pound)
¼   cup minced fresh flat-leaf parsley
2   tablespoons minced fresh oregano
3   tablespoons green olives, coarsely chopped
1½ tablespoons capers
2   teaspoons anchovy paste
⅛   to ¼ teaspoon crushed red pepper
Oregano sprigs (optional)

1. Cook pasta according to package directions, omitting salt and fat.
2. While pasta cooks, heat oil in a nonstick skillet over medium-low heat. Add garlic; sauté 5 minutes. Add tomato and next 6 ingredients. Bring to a boil. Reduce heat to medium; cook 10 minutes or until thick. Combine tomato mixture and pasta, and toss well. Garnish with oregano sprigs, if desired. Yield: 4 servings (serving size: 1½ cups).

Choosing Capers: You'll find capers in the condiment section of your supermarket. The smaller, immature buds are more expensive, but they're also the most intensely flavored. Larger capers (from raisin-size to the size of a small olive) are fine to use, too. We choose small capers when testing our recipes. At any size, capers have an assertive flavor, and you'll find that even a somewhat pricey bottle will last up to a year in the refrigerator. For more tasty ways to use capers, try Caponata with Garlic Crostini, page 18, Roasted Bell Pepper and Olive Pizzas, page 84, and Mediterranean Goat-Cheese Sandwiches, page 178.

prep: 15 minutes ★ cook: 1 hour and 57 minutes ★ other: 10 minutes

FRESH TOMATO LASAGNA

12   uncooked lasagna noodles

Cooking spray

4½ cups chopped onion (about 3)

2   garlic cloves, minced

6   cups chopped seeded peeled tomato
     (about 3½ pounds)

1   cup chopped fresh parsley

2   teaspoons dried oregano

½   teaspoon salt

½   teaspoon dried thyme

½   teaspoon dried marjoram

½   teaspoon pepper

2   (6-ounce) cans Italian-style tomato paste

½   teaspoon dried basil

1   (15-ounce) carton fat-free ricotta cheese

1   (12.3-ounce) package reduced-fat firm tofu, drained

2   cups (8 ounces) shredded sharp provolone cheese

½   cup (2 ounces) grated fresh Romano or Parmesan
     cheese

POINTS value:
8

exchanges:
2½ starch
2 vegetable
1 very lean meat
1 high-fat meat

per serving:
Calories 391
Fat 11.1g (saturated fat 6.3g)
Protein 27.7g
Carbohydrate 49.5g
Fiber 4.4g
Cholesterol 33mg
Iron 4.2mg
Sodium 886mg
Calcium 476mg

1. Cook lasagna according to package directions, omitting salt and fat; drain well.

2. Heat a Dutch oven coated with cooking spray over medium-high heat. Add onion and garlic; cover and cook 5 minutes, stirring occasionally. Add tomato and next 7 ingredients. Bring to a boil; cover, reduce heat, and simmer 45 minutes, stirring occasionally.

3. Preheat oven to 350°.

4. Combine basil, ricotta, and tofu in a bowl; mash ricotta mixture with a potato masher. Spread 2 cups sauce in a 13 x 9-inch baking dish coated with cooking spray. Arrange 3 noodles over sauce; top with 1 cup ricotta mixture, ½ cup provolone cheese, 2 tablespoons Romano, and 1½ cups sauce. Repeat layers twice, ending with noodles. Spread remaining sauce over noodles. Sprinkle with ½ cup provolone cheese and 2 tablespoons Romano. Bake at 350° for 45 minutes. Let stand 10 minutes before serving. Yield: 8 servings.

SPICY TOFU AND NOODLES WITH MUSHROOMS

POINTS value:
6

exchanges:
2 starch
1 lean meat
1½ fat

per serving:
Calories 266
Fat 11.5g (saturated fat 1.2g)
Protein 12.1g
Carbohydrate 30.4g
Fiber 2.6g
Cholesterol 0mg
Iron 3mg
Sodium 326mg
Calcium 175mg

9   cups boiling water, divided
4   ounces uncooked rice vermicelli
1   (0.5-ounce) package dried wood ear or shiitake
     mushrooms
1   tablespoon vegetable oil
½   cup finely chopped onion
½   cup finely chopped carrot
½   cup thinly sliced green onions
2   teaspoons minced peeled fresh ginger
1   teaspoon chile-garlic pepper sauce (such as
     Taste of Thai)
2   garlic cloves, minced
1   tablespoon low-sodium soy sauce
1   tablespoon hoisin sauce
1   teaspoon sugar
2   teaspoons rice vinegar
1   (16-ounce) package firm tofu, drained and cubed
     (about 3 cups)
18   Bibb lettuce leaves
¼   cup hoisin sauce
¼   cup pine nuts, toasted

1. Combine 8 cups boiling water and vermicelli in a bowl; cover and let stand 20 minutes. While vermicelli stands, combine 1 cup boiling water and mushrooms in a bowl; cover and let stand 15 minutes. Drain vermicelli and mushrooms. Chop mushrooms.

2. Heat oil in a large skillet over medium-high heat. Add chopped mushrooms, chopped onion, and next 5 ingredients; sauté 3 minutes. Add soy sauce, 1 tablespoon hoisin sauce, sugar, vinegar, and tofu to pan. Stir in vermicelli, and sauté 2 minutes.

3. Place 3 lettuce leaves on each of 6 plates. Spoon ⅓ cup tofu mixture into each lettuce leaf; drizzle 2 teaspoons hoisin sauce over each serving. Sprinkle each serving with 2 teaspoons pine nuts. Yield: 6 servings.

Meats

DOUBLE CHEESE MEAT LOAF

Two kinds of cheese, tangy mustard, and herbs star in this family favorite. Leftover meat loaf makes great sandwiches for lunch the next day.

POINTS value:
7

exchanges:
1 starch
4 lean meat

per serving:
Calories 290
Fat 10.9g (saturated fat 4.5g)
Protein 32.3g
Carbohydrate 14g
Fiber 0.8g
Cholesterol 124mg
Iron 2.3mg
Sodium 796mg
Calcium 182mg

Cooking spray
1   cup chopped onion
6   tablespoons ketchup, divided
2   tablespoons Dijon mustard, divided
1   cup (4 ounces) preshredded part-skim mozzarella cheese
½   cup Italian-seasoned breadcrumbs
¼   cup chopped fresh parsley
2   tablespoons grated Parmesan cheese
1   teaspoon dried oregano
¼   teaspoon pepper
1   large egg, lightly beaten
1½ pounds ground round

1. Preheat oven to 375°.
2. Heat a medium nonstick skillet coated with cooking spray over medium-high heat. Add onion; sauté 3 minutes. Combine onion, ¼ cup ketchup, 1 tablespoon mustard, mozzarella, and next 6 ingredients in a large bowl. Crumble ground meat over cheese mixture; stir just until blended.
3. Pack meat mixture into an 8 x 4-inch loaf pan coated with cooking spray. Combine 2 tablespoons ketchup and 1 table-spoon mustard; spread over top of loaf. Bake at 375° for 1 hour or until a meat thermometer registers 160°. Let meat loaf stand in pan 10 minutes.
4. Remove meat loaf from pan, and cut into 12 slices.
Yield: 6 servings (serving size: 2 slices).

GREEN PEPPERCORN STEAKS

Drizzled with a flavorful cognac sauce, these tender steaks rest on a bed of peppery watercress. You may substitute ¼ cup less-sodium beef broth for the cognac, if desired, and reduce the salt to ⅛ teaspoon.

3 tablespoons drained brine-packed green peppercorns, crushed
4 (4-ounce) beef tenderloin steaks (about 1 inch thick), trimmed
Cooking spray
2 bunches watercress, trimmed
¼ cup cognac
½ cup less-sodium beef broth
¼ teaspoon salt

1. Gently press crushed green peppercorns into both sides of steaks; let stand at room temperature 20 minutes.
2. Heat a large nonstick skillet coated with cooking spray over medium-high heat. Add watercress; sauté 1 to 2 minutes or until watercress wilts. Remove watercress from pan; set aside, and keep warm.
3. Recoat pan with cooking spray. Add steaks, and cook 6 to 8 minutes on each side or until desired degree of doneness. Remove steaks from pan. Set steaks aside; keep warm.
4. Remove pan from heat; add cognac, beef broth, and salt. Bring to a simmer, and cook 2 to 3 minutes or until sauce is reduced by half.
5. Place watercress on each of 4 plates; place steaks on watercress. Drizzle sauce evenly over steaks and watercress. Yield: 4 servings (serving size: 1 steak and ¼ cup watercress mixture).

POINTS value:
4

exchanges:
3 lean meat

per serving:
Calories 180
Fat 7.6g (saturated fat 3g)
Protein 24.6g
Carbohydrate 1.5g
Fiber 0.7g
Cholesterol 70mg
Iron 1.6mg
Sodium 574mg
Calcium 85mg

Watercress is a member of the mustard family. It has small, crisp, dark-green leaves with a sharp, peppery flavor. Generally, watercress is sold in bunches near the parsley and cilantro in the fresh produce section of the supermarket. If you don't care for the sharp flavor, substitute spinach.

FILET MIGNON WITH MUSHROOM-WINE SAUCE

pictured on page 113

POINTS value:
6

exchanges:
½ starch
3½ lean meat
½ fat

per serving:
Calories 250
Fat 10.7g (saturated fat 3.6g)
Protein 28.5g
Carbohydrate 9.4g
Fiber 0.9g
Cholesterol 84mg
Iron 5.1mg
Sodium 712mg
Calcium 30mg

1   tablespoon butter, divided
⅓   cup finely chopped shallots or green onions
½   pound fresh shiitake mushrooms, stems removed
1½ cups Cabernet Sauvignon or other dry red wine, divided
1   (10½-ounce) can beef consommé, undiluted and divided
Cracked black pepper
4   (4-ounce) beef tenderloin steaks (about 1 inch thick), trimmed
1   tablespoon low-sodium soy sauce
2   teaspoons cornstarch
2   teaspoons minced fresh thyme
Thyme sprigs (optional)

1. Melt 1½ teaspoons butter in a nonstick skillet over medium heat. Add shallots and mushrooms; sauté 4 minutes. Add 1 cup wine and ¾ cup consommé, and cook 5 minutes, stirring frequently. Remove mushrooms with a slotted spoon; place in a bowl. Increase heat to medium-high; cook wine mixture until reduced to ½ cup (about 5 minutes). Add to mushrooms in bowl; set aside. Wipe pan dry with a paper towel.

2. Sprinkle pepper over steaks. Melt 1½ teaspoons butter in pan over medium heat. Add steaks; cook 3 minutes on each side. Reduce heat to medium-low; cook 1½ minutes on each side or until desired degree of doneness. Place on a platter; keep warm.

3. Combine soy sauce and cornstarch. Add ½ cup wine and remaining consommé to pan; scrape pan to loosen browned bits. Bring to a boil; cook 1 minute. Add mushroom mixture, cornstarch mixture, and minced thyme; bring to a boil, and cook 1 minute, stirring constantly. Serve sauce with steaks. Garnish with thyme sprigs, if desired. Yield: 4 servings (serving size: 1 steak and ½ cup sauce).

PORCINI-CRUSTED BEEF TENDERLOIN WITH WILD-MUSHROOM SAUCE

Before being seared, the tenderloin is dusted with a dried mushroom powder that imparts a rustic, earthy flavor. Serve with a full-bodied red wine.

2   cups boiling water
1½   cups dried porcini mushrooms (about 1½ ounces), divided
1   (2-pound) center-cut beef tenderloin, trimmed
¾   teaspoon salt, divided
¼   teaspoon white pepper, divided
2   teaspoons vegetable oil
Cooking spray
2   tablespoons chilled butter, cut into small pieces

1. Combine boiling water and 1 cup mushrooms in a bowl; cover and let stand 30 minutes.
2. Preheat oven to 400°.
3. While 1 cup mushrooms stand, place ½ cup mushrooms in a blender; process until finely ground. Sprinkle beef with ground mushrooms, ½ teaspoon salt, and ⅛ teaspoon pepper. Heat oil in large nonstick skillet over medium-high heat. Add beef; cook 5 minutes, browning on all sides. Place beef on a broiler pan coated with cooking spray. Insert meat thermometer into thickest portion of beef. Bake at 400° for 30 minutes or until meat thermometer registers 145° (medium-rare) to 160° (medium). Place tenderloin on a platter; cover with foil. Let stand 10 minutes.
4. While tenderloin stands, drain hydrated mushrooms through a cheesecloth-lined sieve into a medium saucepan, reserving soaking liquid; coarsely chop mushrooms. Bring reserved soaking liquid to a boil, and add chopped mushrooms. Reduce heat, and simmer until reduced to 1 cup (about 12 minutes). Add ¼ teaspoon salt, ⅛ teaspoon pepper, and butter, stirring with a whisk until butter melts. Serve with tenderloin. Yield: 8 servings (serving size: 5 ounces meat and 2 tablespoons sauce).

POINTS value:
5

exchanges:
½ vegetable
3 lean meat
1 fat

per serving:
Calories 226
Fat 12g (saturated fat 5.1g)
Protein 24.6g
Carbohydrate 4.1g
Fiber 0.6g
Cholesterol 79mg
Iron 3.1mg
Sodium 303mg
Calcium 8mg

BEEF TENDERLOIN WITH CILANTRO SAUCE

POINTS **value:**
5

exchanges:
2 vegetable
2 medium-fat meat

per serving:
Calories 213
Fat 9.3g (saturated fat 2.9g)
Protein 20.2g
Carbohydrate 11.5g
Fiber 1.4g
Cholesterol 57mg
Iron 2.8mg
Sodium 375mg
Calcium 30mg

2	tablespoons minced fresh cilantro
2	tablespoons minced fresh onion
2	tablespoons minced red bell pepper
3	tablespoons vegetable broth (such as Swanson)
1	tablespoon white vinegar
1	tablespoon extravirgin olive oil
¼	teaspoon salt
¼	teaspoon dried oregano
¼	teaspoon crushed red pepper
⅛	teaspoon black pepper
1	garlic clove, minced

Cooking spray

4	cups sliced onion
½	teaspoon sugar
1	(1½-pound) center-cut beef tenderloin
½	teaspoon salt
½	teaspoon garlic powder
½	teaspoon dried oregano
½	teaspoon black pepper
¼	teaspoon ground cumin

1. Combine first 11 ingredients in a bowl, stirring with a whisk until well blended. Set sauce aside.

2. Heat a large skillet coated with cooking spray over medium heat. Add sliced onion and sugar; cover and cook 10 minutes or until golden brown, stirring frequently. Keep warm.

3. Prepare broiler.

4. Cut tenderloin lengthwise with grain into 6 even steaks. Place 1 steak between 2 sheets of heavy-duty plastic wrap; flatten to an even thickness using a meat mallet or rolling pin. Repeat procedure with remaining steaks.

5. Combine salt and next 4 ingredients; rub over both sides of steaks. Place on a broiler pan coated with cooking spray. Broil 2 minutes on each side or until desired degree of doneness. Top steaks with onion mixture; drizzle with sauce. Yield: 6 servings (serving size: 1 steak, ½ cup onion mixture, and 4 teaspoons sauce).

KOREAN-STYLE FLANK STEAK

1 (1½-pound) flank steak, trimmed
¼ cup finely chopped green onions
¼ cup low-sodium soy sauce
2 tablespoons sugar
2 tablespoons dry sherry (optional)
1 tablespoon dark sesame oil
1 tablespoon water
¼ teaspoon coarsely ground black pepper
4 garlic cloves, minced
Cooking spray

1. Combine first 9 ingredients in a large zip-top plastic bag. Seal bag; marinate in refrigerator 8 hours, turning bag occasionally.

2. Preheat broiler.

3. Remove steak from bag, reserving marinade. Place steak on a broiler pan coated with cooking spray; brush with reserved marinade. Broil 8 minutes; turn steak, and brush with marinade. Broil 8 minutes or until desired degree of doneness; discard remaining marinade. Cut steak diagonally across grain into thin slices. Yield: 6 servings (serving size: 3 ounces).

POINTS value:
6

exchanges:
3½ lean meat
1 fat

per serving:
Calories 231
Fat 14g (saturated fat 5.6g)
Protein 22g
Carbohydrate 3.1g
Fiber 0.1g
Cholesterol 60mg
Iron 2.3mg
Sodium 233mg
Calcium 10mg

TEXAS-GRILLED SIRLOIN WITH FRESH TOMATO SALSA

pictured on page 3

POINTS value:
4

exchanges:
1 vegetable
3 lean meat

per serving:
Calories 177
Fat 7.1g (saturated fat 2.6g)
Protein 19.6g
Carbohydrate 8.8g
Fiber 1.6g
Cholesterol 49mg
Iron 2.4mg
Sodium 202mg
Calcium 31mg

1   pound lean boneless top sirloin steak, trimmed
¼   cup fresh lime juice
2   tablespoons chopped fresh oregano
1   tablespoon chopped fresh rosemary
1   teaspoon sugar
1   teaspoon ground red pepper
1   teaspoon black pepper
1   large garlic clove, crushed
2   cups chopped tomato
¼   cup chopped green onions
1   tablespoon finely chopped fresh cilantro
1   tablespoon fresh lime juice
1   teaspoon minced fresh jalapeño pepper
¼   teaspoon salt
Cooking spray
Lime wedges (optional)
Cilantro sprigs (optional)

1. Combine first 8 ingredients in a large zip-top plastic bag; seal bag, and shake well. Marinate in refrigerator at least 8 hours, turning bag occasionally.
2. While meat marinates, combine tomato and next 5 ingredients in a medium bowl; stir well. Cover and chill at least 3 hours.
3. Prepare grill.
4. Remove steak from bag; discard marinade. Place steak on grill rack coated with cooking spray; cover and grill 5 to 6 minutes on each side or until desired degree of doneness. Let steak stand 5 minutes. Cut diagonally across grain into thin slices. Serve with salsa. Garnish with lime wedges and cilantro sprigs, if desired. Yield: 4 servings (serving size: 3 ounces meat and ½ cup salsa).

VEAL IN LIME CREAM SAUCE

Lime zest and juice add a citrus tang to veal cutlets—a pleasant departure from the more traditional flavor pairings of Marsala or Parmesan cheese and tomato.

1	pound veal cutlets (¼ inch thick)
¼	teaspoon salt
¼	teaspoon freshly ground black pepper
	Butter-flavored cooking spray
1	large lime
2	tablespoons dry white wine or fat-free, less-sodium chicken broth
1	tablespoon plus 1 teaspoon all-purpose flour
½	cup fat-free, less-sodium chicken broth
⅔	cup evaporated fat-free milk

1. Sprinkle veal cutlets with salt and pepper. Heat a large nonstick skillet coated with cooking spray over medium-high heat. Add cutlets, and cook 1 minute on each side or until browned. Remove from pan; set aside, and keep warm.
2. Remove zest and 2 tablespoons juice from lime. Set zest aside. Add lime juice and wine to pan; cook over high heat 1 minute or until mixture is reduced by half. Combine flour, broth, and milk; stir well. Add to lime juice mixture. Cook over medium heat 5 minutes or until thick and bubbly, stirring constantly. Return cutlets to pan; cook until thoroughly heated. Sprinkle with lime zest, and serve immediately. Yield: 4 servings (serving size: 3 ounces meat and ¼ cup sauce).

***POINTS* value:**
5

exchanges:
3 lean meat
1 fat

per serving:
Calories 218
Fat 6.1g (saturated fat 1.6g)
Protein 31g
Carbohydrate 8.1g
Fiber 0.1g
Cholesterol 102mg
Iron 1.2mg
Sodium 282mg
Calcium 118mg

MARINATED LAMB CHOPS WITH HERBS

Next time you're setting a table for two, try these lamb chops marinated in robust red wine, soy sauce, and fresh herbs. Complete the meal with couscous and steamed carrots.

POINTS value:
6

exchanges:
4 lean meat

per serving:
Calories 237
Fat 12.4g (saturated fat 4.4g)
Protein 27.3g
Carbohydrate 2.6g
Fiber 0.2g
Cholesterol 86mg
Iron 2.8mg
Sodium 567mg
Calcium 28mg

¼ cup dry red wine
2 tablespoons chopped fresh mint
2 tablespoons low-sodium soy sauce
1½ teaspoons chopped fresh rosemary
½ teaspoon coarsely ground black pepper
1 garlic clove, crushed
4 (3-ounce) lean lamb rib chops, trimmed

1. Combine first 6 ingredients in a large zip-top plastic bag. Add chops; seal bag, and marinate in refrigerator 8 hours, turning bag occasionally. Remove chops from bag, reserving marinade.
2. Prepare grill or broiler.
3. Place chops on grill rack or broiler pan, and cook 4 minutes on each side or until desired degree of doneness, basting occasionally with reserved marinade. Yield: 2 servings (serving size: 2 chops).

Lamb: Today, lamb is leaner than ever. And because lamb cuts are leaner, it's very important that you watch the cooking time and temperature carefully, or the meat will be overcooked and tough. For the best flavor and tenderness, cook lamb only until it's slightly pink: medium-rare (145°) or medium (160°). If you cook the meat to 180° or 185° (well done), it will be tough and dry.

PORK AND PEAR SAUTÉ WITH LEMON–VODKA SAUCE

The pan-seared pear halves provide a touch of elegance to this simple entrée while the vodka adds unique flavor to the sauce.

2	teaspoons olive oil, divided
2	(4-ounce) boneless center-cut loin pork chops (about ¾ inch thick), trimmed
½	teaspoon salt, divided
½	teaspoon cracked black pepper, divided
2	Anjou pears (about 1 pound), peeled, cored, and halved
¼	cup vodka or dry white wine
2	teaspoons grated lemon rind
1	tablespoon fresh lemon juice
1	tablespoon chopped fresh chives

1. Heat 1 teaspoon olive oil in a large nonstick skillet over medium heat. Sprinkle pork chops with ¼ teaspoon salt and ¼ teaspoon pepper. Add pork chops to pan; sauté 3 minutes on each side or until pork is done. Remove pork from pan, and keep warm.

2. Heat 1 teaspoon oil in pan over medium heat. Place pear halves in pan, cut sides down. Cook 2 minutes on each side or until golden. Remove pear halves from pan, and keep warm. Stir in vodka, scraping pan to loosen browned bits. Stir in ¼ teaspoon salt, ¼ teaspoon pepper, rind, juice, and chives, and cook 1 minute. Serve with pork chops and pears. Yield: 2 servings (serving size: 1 pork chop, 2 pear halves, and 1 tablespoon sauce).

POINTS value:
7

exchanges:
2 fruit
3 medium-fat meat

per serving:
Calories 338
Fat 13.3g (saturated fat 3.2g)
Protein 25.9g
Carbohydrate 30.5g
Fiber 4.9g
Cholesterol 71mg
Iron 1.6mg
Sodium 661mg
Calcium 34mg

BARBECUED PORK CHOPS

Serve up a true blue-plate special when you pair these tender chops with Stovetop "Baked Beans" (page 152) and sautéed apples.

POINTS value:
6

exchanges:
½ starch
3½ lean meat

per serving:
Calories 244
Fat 11.3g (saturated fat 3.9g)
Protein 24.6g
Carbohydrate 9.9g
Fiber 0.2g
Cholesterol 77mg
Iron 1.5mg
Sodium 649mg
Calcium 22mg

¼ cup packed brown sugar
¼ cup ketchup
1 tablespoon Worcestershire sauce
1 tablespoon low-sodium soy sauce
1 teaspoon dried thyme
1 teaspoon garlic salt
¼ teaspoon ground red pepper
6 (6-ounce) bone-in center-cut pork chops (about ½ inch thick), trimmed

Cooking spray

1. Prepare grill or broiler.
2. Combine first 4 ingredients in a small bowl. Place ¼ cup sauce in a small bowl, and set aside.
3. Combine thyme, garlic salt, and pepper; sprinkle over pork chops. Place pork chops on grill rack or broiler pan coated with cooking spray; cook 6 minutes on each side, basting with remaining sauce. Serve pork chops with reserved ¼ cup sauce. Yield: 6 servings (serving size: 1 pork chop and about 2 teaspoons sauce).

Perfect Pork: Cook pork to 150° to 155°. Perfect pork will have a faint pink color. For bone-in and boneless chops, each chop needs to be the thickness called for in the recipe. If they're thicker, they won't get done in the time specified in the recipe; if thinner, they'll be overcooked. Let larger cuts of pork, roasts, and tenderloins stand for 10 to 15 minutes after cooking to reabsorb juices and to allow the meat to finish cooking (raising the internal temperature by 5° to 10°). The United States Department of Agriculture (USDA) recommends cooking pork to 160°.

prep: 6 minutes ★ **cook:** 3 to 4 hours ★ **other:** 8 hours and 10 minutes

MAPLE-GLAZED BOURBON PORK ROAST

Fragrant hickory smoke seasons and tenderizes this succulent pork roast.

4	(3-inch) chunks hickory wood
1	cup maple syrup
⅔	cup bourbon
1	teaspoon coarsely ground black pepper
⅛	teaspoon ground red pepper
1	(3-pound) boneless pork loin roast, trimmed, rolled and tied
4	sage sprigs
Cooking spray	

1. Soak hickory wood chunks in water 1 to 24 hours. Drain well.

2. Combine syrup, bourbon, and peppers in a large zip-top plastic bag. Add roast; seal bag, and marinate in refrigerator 8 hours, turning bag occasionally. Remove roast from bag, reserving marinade. Refrigerate ⅔ cup marinade.

3. Prepare charcoal fire in meat smoker; let burn 15 to 20 minutes. Place hickory chunks on top of coals. Place water pan in smoker; add remaining reserved marinade and sage sprigs. Add hot tap water to fill pan.

4. Place roast on rack coated with cooking spray in smoker. Insert meat thermometer into thickest portion of roast. Cover with smoker lid; cook 3 to 4 hours or until thermometer registers 155° (slightly pink). Refill water pan with water, and add additional charcoal to fire as needed.

5. Remove roast from smoker; cover and let stand 10 minutes. Place remaining ⅔ cup marinade in a small saucepan. Bring to a boil; remove from heat. Cut roast into thin slices; serve with hot marinade. Yield: 12 servings (serving size: 3 ounces meat and about 1 tablespoon sauce).

POINTS **value:**
5

exchanges:
½ starch
3½ lean meat

per serving:
Calories 224
Fat 11.4g (saturated fat 3.9g)
Protein 21.8g
Carbohydrate 7.1g
Fiber 0g
Cholesterol 74mg
Iron 1.1mg
Sodium 57mg
Calcium 15mg

HONEY-MUSTARD PORK TENDERLOIN WITH KALE

pictured on facing page

POINTS value:
6

exchanges:
1 starch
1 vegetable
3 lean meat

per serving:
Calories 287
Fat 5.2g (saturated fat 1.1g)
Protein 28.6g
Carbohydrate 31.5g
Fiber 1.8g
Cholesterol 74mg
Iron 3.8mg
Sodium 634mg
Calcium 175mg

1	(1-pound) pork tenderloin, trimmed
¼	cup stone-ground mustard
2	tablespoons honey
1	tablespoon sherry vinegar or white wine vinegar
Cooking spray	
¾	cup fat-free, less-sodium chicken broth
¼	cup sherry or fat-free, less-sodium chicken broth
2	tablespoons minced shallots
2	tablespoons honey
1	tablespoon sherry vinegar or white wine vinegar
1	tablespoon stone-ground mustard
6	cups torn kale
¼	cup fat-free, less-sodium chicken broth
1	tablespoon minced shallots
1	tablespoon stone-ground mustard

1. Combine first 4 ingredients in a large zip-top plastic bag. Seal bag, and marinate in refrigerator 2 hours, turning bag occasionally. Remove pork from bag, reserving marinade.
2. Preheat oven to 375°.
3. Place pork on a broiler pan coated with cooking spray. Insert meat thermometer into thickest portion of pork. Bake at 375° for 40 minutes or until thermometer registers 155° (slightly pink). Cover pork and let stand 10 minutes before slicing.
4. While pork cooks, combine reserved marinade, ¾ cup chicken broth, and next 5 ingredients in a small saucepan; bring to a boil. Reduce heat to medium; cook 15 minutes. Set aside.
5. While pork stands, combine kale, ¼ cup chicken broth, 1 tablespoon shallots, and 1 tablespoon mustard in a large skillet over medium heat. Cover and cook 8 minutes or until tender, stirring occasionally. Yield: 4 servings (serving size: 3 ounces meat, 3 tablespoons sauce, and ½ cup kale).

Honey-Mustard Pork Tenderloin with Kale

Filet Mignon with Mushroom-Wine Sauce, page 102

Mussels Marinara, page 74

Pasta Puttanesca, page 96

Pasta Primavera

PASTA PRIMAVERA
pictured on facing page

To keep the prosciutto from sticking together in the pasta, lay it out to dry on a plate after you chop it. Nutty, rich Asiago cheese complements the saltiness of the prosciutto, but fresh Parmesan can be substituted.

12	ounces uncooked spaghettini or vermicelli
2½	cups (3-inch) diagonally sliced asparagus (about 1 pound)
1½	cups shelled green peas (about 1½ pounds unshelled)
1	tablespoon olive oil, divided
2	cups diced zucchini
½	cup sliced green onions
1	cup fat-free, less-sodium chicken broth
⅓	cup dry white wine or fat-free, less-sodium chicken broth
2	tablespoons minced fresh basil
2	tablespoons minced fresh oregano
½	teaspoon kosher salt or ¼ teaspoon table salt
¼	teaspoon black pepper
2	ounces thinly sliced prosciutto or ham, chopped
¾	cup (3 ounces) grated Asiago or fresh Parmesan cheese

POINTS value:
5

exchanges:
2 starch
2 vegetable
1 medium-fat meat

per serving:
Calories 269
Fat 6.2g (saturated fat 2.4g)
Protein 13.8g
Carbohydrate 40g
Fiber 3.2g
Cholesterol 15mg
Iron 3.1mg
Sodium 448mg
Calcium 154mg

1. Bring water to a boil in a large Dutch oven. Add pasta; cook 5 minutes. Add asparagus, and cook 2 minutes. Add peas, and cook 1 minute. Drain well, and set aside.

2. Heat 2 teaspoons oil in a large nonstick skillet over medium-high heat. Add zucchini; sauté 5 minutes. Add green onions; sauté 1 minute. Add broth and wine; bring to a boil. Stir in pasta mixture, basil, and oregano; cook 1 minute. Remove from heat; stir in 1 teaspoon oil, salt, pepper, and prosciutto. Spoon 1¼ cups primavera into each of 8 shallow bowls; top each serving with 1½ tablespoons cheese. Yield: 8 servings.

OVERNIGHT ARTICHOKE AND HAM STRATA

POINTS value:
6

exchanges:
2 starch
2 very lean meat
1 lean meat

per serving:
Calories 280
Fat 8.9g (saturated fat 4.1g)
Protein 20.4g
Carbohydrate 29.8g
Fiber 0.1g
Cholesterol 133mg
Iron 2.3mg
Sodium 819mg
Calcium 367mg

3   (2-ounce) English muffins, split and quartered
Cooking spray
1   tablespoon butter, melted
1   cup chopped lean ham (about 4 ounces)
½   cup (2 ounces) grated fresh Parmesan cheese
2   tablespoons chopped fresh chives
1   (14-ounce) can artichoke hearts, drained and chopped
3   large garlic cloves, minced
⅛   teaspoon ground nutmeg
1   (12-ounce) can evaporated fat-free milk
3   large eggs
3   large egg whites

1. Arrange muffin pieces, crust sides down, in an 8-inch square baking dish coated with cooking spray, and drizzle with butter. Arrange ham and next 4 ingredients over muffin pieces.
2. Combine nutmeg and next 3 ingredients in a bowl; stir well with a whisk. Pour over muffin mixture. Cover; chill 8 hours or overnight.
3. Preheat oven to 375°.
4. Uncover strata; bake at 375° for 50 minutes or until set. Let stand 10 minutes. Yield: 6 servings.

Make-Ahead Tip: Prepare the strata a day ahead; cover and chill 8 hours or overnight. When you're ready to cook the strata, just take it out of the refrigerator, uncover, and bake in a preheated oven.

Poultry

prep: 15 minutes ★ **cook:** 1 hour

SPICED CHICKEN IN CREAMY ALMOND SAUCE

POINTS value:
6

exchanges:
½ starch
6 very lean meat

per serving:
Calories 304
Fat 7.9g (saturated fat 1.3g)
Protein 46.9g
Carbohydrate 8.7g
Fiber 2.1g
Cholesterol 110mg
Iron 2.4mg
Sodium 410mg
Calcium 60mg

1 tablespoon olive oil
6 (3-inch) cinnamon sticks
5 bay leaves
1½ cups finely chopped onion
6 garlic cloves, minced
2 teaspoons curry powder
½ teaspoon ground turmeric
½ teaspoon salt
¼ teaspoon ground cardamom
2½ pounds skinless, boneless chicken breast, cut into 1-inch pieces
1 cup fat-free, less-sodium chicken broth
¼ cup fat-free sour cream
1 teaspoon all-purpose flour
½ teaspoon sugar
¼ cup slivered almonds, toasted and ground
⅓ cup chopped red bell pepper
2 tablespoons slivered almonds, toasted

1. Heat oil in a large nonstick skillet over medium heat. Add cinnamon sticks and bay leaves. Cook 2 minutes or until fragrant. Add onion and garlic; sauté 5 minutes or until tender. Add curry powder, turmeric, salt, and cardamom. Add chicken and broth; bring to a boil. Cover, reduce heat, and simmer 35 minutes or until chicken is tender.
2. Remove chicken from pan with a slotted spoon. Cook liquid in pan over low heat 5 minutes. Combine sour cream, flour, and sugar in a bowl; stir in ½ cup hot liquid. Add sour cream mixture to pan; stir until smooth. Return chicken to pan; stir in ground almonds. Cook 5 minutes or until thick, stirring frequently. Sprinkle with bell pepper. Discard cinnamon sticks and bay leaves. Sprinkle with slivered almonds. Yield: 6 servings (serving size: about 1 cup chicken mixture and 1 teaspoon almonds).

RASPBERRY-BALSAMIC CHICKEN

Other fruit preserves, such as apricot, blackberry, or peach,
will also work in this recipe.

1	teaspoon vegetable oil
½	cup chopped red onion
1½	teaspoons minced fresh thyme
½	teaspoon salt, divided
4	(6-ounce) skinless, boneless chicken breast halves
⅓	cup seedless raspberry preserves
2	tablespoons balsamic vinegar
¼	teaspoon pepper

POINTS value:
6

exchanges:
1½ starch
5 very lean meat

per serving:
Calories 278
Fat 3.3g (saturated fat 0.7g)
Protein 39.5g
Carbohydrate 20.7g
Fiber 0.4g
Cholesterol 99mg
Iron 1.4mg
Sodium 408mg
Calcium 27mg

1. Heat oil in a large nonstick skillet over medium-high heat. Add onion; sauté 5 minutes. Combine thyme and ¼ teaspoon salt; sprinkle over chicken. Add chicken to pan; cook 6 minutes on each side or until done. Remove chicken from pan; keep warm.

2. Reduce heat to medium. Add ¼ teaspoon salt, preserves, vinegar, and pepper, stirring constantly until preserves melt. Spoon raspberry sauce over chicken, and serve immediately. Yield: 4 servings (serving size: 1 chicken breast half and 2 tablespoons sauce).

Balsamic Vinegar: The best balsamic vinegars to use for cooking are labeled *condimento balsamico* and are reasonably priced. They have a slightly more acidic, but no less complex, nature than other vinegars. Aged for shorter periods and by slightly different methods, these vinegars are still quite tasty.

GREEK FETA CHICKEN

A seasoned yogurt mixture tenderizes and flavors the chicken as it marinates; then it becomes a sauce for the chicken as it broils.

POINTS value:
5

exchanges:
½ skim milk
5 very lean meat

per serving:
Calories 253
Fat 5.2g (saturated fat 2.7g)
Protein 43.9g
Carbohydrate 6.3g
Fiber 0.2g
Cholesterol 113mg
Iron 1.6mg
Sodium 303mg
Calcium 172mg

1 (8-ounce) carton plain low-fat yogurt
1 tablespoon lemon juice
½ teaspoon dried oregano
½ teaspoon dried rosemary
¼ teaspoon pepper
1 large garlic clove, minced
4 (6-ounce) skinless, boneless chicken breast halves
Cooking spray
¼ cup (2 ounces) crumbled feta cheese
1 tablespoon chopped fresh parsley

1. Combine first 6 ingredients in a large zip-top plastic bag; add chicken. Seal bag, and shake until chicken is well coated. Marinate in refrigerator 30 minutes.
2. Preheat broiler.
3. Remove chicken from bag, reserving marinade. Place chicken on a broiler pan coated with cooking spray. Broil 7 minutes. Turn chicken over. Spoon reserved marinade over chicken; top with feta cheese. Broil 7 minutes or until chicken is done. Sprinkle with parsley. Yield: 4 servings (serving size: 1 chicken breast half).

Easy Cleanup: For easier cleanup, use zip-top plastic bags to marinate the chicken, and line the broiler pan with foil. Discard the plastic bag and foil, leaving only the broiler rack to wash.

prep: 8 minutes ★ **cook:** 12 minutes

ITALIAN CHICKEN AND VEGETABLES

You'll get rave reviews when you serve this light and tangy chicken.
It's a healthy one-dish meal.

1	teaspoon garlic powder
½	teaspoon salt, divided
¼	teaspoon pepper, divided
4	(6-ounce) skinless, boneless chicken breast halves
Cooking spray	
1	tablespoon olive oil
1	(8-ounce) package presliced mushrooms
1	small zucchini, quartered lengthwise and sliced
4	garlic cloves, minced
1	cup chopped plum tomato (about 3 tomatoes)
½	cup chopped red onion
½	cup chopped fresh basil
4	teaspoons balsamic vinegar
¼	cup (1 ounce) grated fresh Parmesan cheese

POINTS value:
6

exchanges:
2 vegetable
6 very lean meat

per serving:
Calories 293
Fat 7.9g (saturated fat 2.3g)
Protein 45.2g
Carbohydrate 9.5g
Fiber 2.2g
Cholesterol 105mg
Iron 2.2mg
Sodium 524mg
Calcium 129mg

1. Preheat broiler.

2. Combine garlic powder, ¼ teaspoon salt, and ⅛ teaspoon pepper in a small bowl; sprinkle chicken with garlic powder mixture. Place chicken on a broiler pan coated with cooking spray, and broil 6 minutes on each side or until chicken is done.

3. While chicken cooks, heat olive oil in a large nonstick skillet over medium-high heat. Add ¼ teaspoon salt, mushrooms, zucchini, and minced garlic; sauté 2 minutes. Add ⅛ teaspoon pepper, tomato, onion, basil, and vinegar; sauté 3 minutes. Serve vegetable mixture over chicken; sprinkle with cheese. Yield: 4 servings (serving size: 1 chicken breast half, ½ cup vegetables, and 1 tablespoon cheese).

SEARED CHICKEN AND PEPPERS WITH CILANTRO SAUCE

Bold flavors and fresh ingredients take the humble chicken breast from ordinary fare to the ultimate hero of the dinner table.

POINTS value:
5

exchanges:
2 vegetable
5 very lean meat

per serving:
Calories 254
Fat 5.9g (saturated fat 1.1g)
Protein 40.5g
Carbohydrate 7.5g
Fiber 0.5g
Cholesterol 99mg
Iron 1.7mg
Sodium 574mg
Calcium 30mg

½ cup picante sauce
4 (6-ounce) skinless, boneless chicken breast halves
1 red bell pepper, quartered lengthwise
1 yellow bell pepper, quartered lengthwise
1 garlic clove, peeled
1 jalapeño pepper, seeded
1½ cups fresh cilantro leaves
1 tablespoon olive oil
1½ teaspoons all-purpose flour
⅓ cup fat-free, less-sodium chicken broth
¼ teaspoon salt
Cooking spray
Cilantro sprigs (optional)

1. Combine first 4 ingredients in a large zip-top plastic bag; seal bag, and marinate in refrigerator 20 minutes.
2. While chicken marinates, drop garlic and jalapeño pepper through food chute with food processor on, and process until minced. Add cilantro leaves; process until finely minced. Heat oil in a small saucepan over medium heat. Add flour; cook 1 minute, stirring constantly with a whisk. Add cilantro mixture, broth, and salt; cook 4 minutes or until slightly thick, stirring occasionally. Remove from heat; keep warm.
3. Prepare grill or broiler.
4. Remove chicken and bell pepper pieces from bag, and reserve marinade. Place chicken and bell pepper pieces on grill rack or broiler pan coated with cooking spray. Cook 5 minutes on each side or until chicken is done, basting with marinade. Place cilantro sauce on each of 4 plates. Arrange chicken and bell pepper pieces on top of sauce. Garnish with cilantro sprigs, if desired. Yield: 4 servings (serving size: 1 chicken breast half, 2 bell pepper pieces, and about 1 tablespoon sauce).

prep: 25 minutes ★ **cook:** 34 minutes

ARTICHOKE-AND-GOAT CHEESE-STUFFED CHICKEN BREASTS

Stuffed chicken breasts never fail to impress. Follow these easy instructions to master a not-so-tricky technique, and then sit back and listen to your guests rave about the meal.

1	(14-ounce) can artichoke bottoms
½	cup (2 ounces) crumbled goat or feta cheese
¼	cup chopped fresh chives, divided
1½	teaspoons chopped fresh thyme, divided
1½	teaspoons grated lemon rind, divided
8	(6-ounce) skinless, boneless chicken breast halves
¼	teaspoon pepper
2	teaspoons olive oil, divided
1	teaspoon cornstarch
2	tablespoons fresh lemon juice

POINTS value:
5

exchanges:
1 vegetable
6 very lean meat

per serving:
Calories 251
Fat 5.8g (saturated fat 2.5g)
Protein 42.7g
Carbohydrate 4.6g
Fiber 0.7g
Cholesterol 106mg
Iron 2.1mg
Sodium 280mg
Calcium 85mg

1. Drain artichokes, reserving liquid. Coarsely chop artichoke bottoms. Combine artichokes, goat cheese, 2 tablespoons chives, 1 teaspoon thyme, and 1 teaspoon lemon rind in a medium bowl; stir well.

2. Cut a horizontal slit through thickest portion of each chicken breast half to form a pocket. Stuff about ¼ cup artichoke mixture into each pocket. Sprinkle chicken with pepper.

3. Heat 1 teaspoon oil in a large skillet over medium-high heat. Add 4 chicken breast halves; cook 6 to 8 minutes on each side or until chicken is done. Remove chicken from pan; keep warm. Repeat procedure with 1 teaspoon oil and 4 chicken breast halves. Add reserved artichoke liquid, ½ teaspoon thyme, and ½ teaspoon lemon rind to pan. Combine cornstarch and lemon juice; add to pan. Bring to a boil; cook 1 minute, stirring constantly. Return chicken to pan. Cover and simmer 2 minutes or until thoroughly heated. Spoon sauce over chicken. Top with 2 tablespoons chives. Yield: 8 servings (serving size: 1 chicken breast half and 1 tablespoon sauce).

OVEN–FRIED CHICKEN

pictured on page 135

Double-dipping gives this chicken more crunchy coating. There are chicken breasts or thighs for the adults and drumsticks for the kids. Serve with cole slaw.

POINTS value:
7

exchanges:
1½ starch
5 very lean meat
1 fat

per serving:
Calories 342
Fat 9.2g (saturated fat 2.9g)
Protein 40.6g
Carbohydrate 21.1g
Fiber 1g
Cholesterol 110mg
Iron 3.5mg
Sodium 381mg
Calcium 36mg

1   cup egg substitute
1½ cups all–purpose flour
1   teaspoon garlic powder
1   teaspoon paprika
½   teaspoon salt
½   teaspoon dried thyme
¼   teaspoon white pepper
3   chicken breast halves (about 1½ pounds), skinned
3   chicken drumsticks (about ¾ pound), skinned
3   chicken thighs (about ¾ pound), skinned
Cooking spray
1   tablespoon butter, melted

1. Preheat oven to 400°.

2. Place egg substitute in a shallow dish. Combine flour and next 5 ingredients in a shallow dish. Dip chicken pieces in egg substitute, and dredge in flour mixture. Dip and dredge each piece a second time.

3. Arrange chicken on a jelly-roll pan coated with cooking spray. Drizzle butter over chicken. Bake at 400° for 50 minutes or until done. Yield: 6 servings (serving size: 1 breast half or 1 thigh and 1 drumstick).

prep: 8 minutes ★ **cook:** 40 minutes ★ **other:** 1 hour

LEMON–GARLIC CHICKEN THIGHS

Chicken thighs roast in a tangy-sweet marinade, creating a richly flavored sauce.
A side of couscous is ideal for soaking up the sauce.

¼	cup fresh lemon juice
2	tablespoons molasses
2	teaspoons Worcestershire sauce
4	garlic cloves, chopped
8	chicken thighs (about 2 pounds), skinned

Cooking spray

¼	teaspoon salt
¼	teaspoon pepper

1. Combine first 4 ingredients in a large zip-top plastic bag; add chicken. Seal bag, and marinate in refrigerator at least 1 hour.
2. Preheat oven to 425°.
3. Remove chicken from bag; reserve marinade. Arrange chicken in a shallow roasting pan coated with cooking spray. Pour reserved marinade over chicken, and sprinkle with salt and pepper. Bake at 425° for 20 minutes; baste chicken with marinade. Bake an additional 20 minutes or until chicken is done. Yield: 4 servings (serving size: 2 chicken thighs).

Chicken Thighs: Thighs have a slightly higher fat content than the oh-so-lean breast. But dark meat with the skin removed has less total fat than the same amount of beef sirloin or tenderloin, a pork chop, or a portion of salmon.

POINTS value:
6

exchanges:
4½ lean meat

per serving:
Calories 258
Fat 11.6g (saturated fat 3.3g)
Protein 27.3g
Carbohydrate 9.9g
Fiber 0.1g
Cholesterol 98mg
Iron 1.9mg
Sodium 268mg
Calcium 43mg

prep: 18 minutes ★ **cook:** 1 hour

ROASTED LEMON CHICKEN WITH POTATOES

pictured on page 134

POINTS value:
7

exchanges:
2 starch
4 lean meat

per serving:
Calories 349
Fat 11.4g (saturated fat 2.4g)
Protein 36.9g
Carbohydrate 25.9g
Fiber 3g
Cholesterol 141mg
Iron 4mg
Sodium 539mg
Calcium 69mg

1	tablespoon olive oil, divided
1	large lemon, thinly sliced
½	teaspoon grated lemon rind
1	tablesoon fresh lemon juice
½	teaspoon salt, divided
¼	teaspoon freshly ground black pepper, divided
6	garlic cloves, minced and divided
8	(3-ounce) skinless, boneless chicken thighs
1	teaspoon chopped fresh or ¼ teaspoon dried rosemary
12	grape or cherry tomatoes
12	kalamata olives
8	small red potatoes, quartered

Rosemary sprigs (optional)

1. Preheat oven to 450°.

2. Brush a 10-inch cast-iron skillet with 1 teaspoon olive oil. Arrange lemon slices in a single layer in bottom of pan.

3. Combine 1 teaspoon olive oil, lemon rind, lemon juice, ¼ teaspoon salt, ⅛ teaspoon pepper, and 4 minced garlic cloves in a large bowl. Add chicken; toss to coat. Arrange chicken in a single layer over lemon slices; drizzle with remaining lemon juice mixture.

4. Combine 1 teaspoon olive oil, ¼ teaspoon salt, ⅛ teaspoon pepper, remaining minced garlic cloves, rosemary, tomatoes, olives, and potatoes in a bowl; toss to coat. Arrange potato mixture over chicken; drizzle with remaining olive oil mixture. Bake at 450° for 1 hour or until chicken is done and potatoes are tender. Garnish with rosemary sprigs, if desired. Yield: 4 servings (serving size: 2 chicken thighs, 3 tomatoes, 3 olives, and 8 potato wedges).

128 Poultry

prep: 25 minutes ★ **cook:** 1 hour and 15 minutes ★ **other:** 10 minutes

BISTRO ROAST CHICKEN

Serve the roasted heads of garlic on the side, or squeeze out the pulp, and use it as a spread on baguette slices.

2	chicken leg quarters (about 1½ pounds)
1	tablespoon chopped fresh basil
1	tablespoon chopped fresh thyme
1	tablespoon chopped fresh rosemary
2	teaspoons olive oil
½	teaspoon salt
¼	teaspoon pepper
2	whole garlic heads

1. Preheat oven to 375°.

2. Rinse chicken under cold water; pat dry. Trim excess fat. Loosen skin from thigh and leg by inserting fingers, gently pushing between skin and meat. Combine basil and next 5 ingredients. Rub herb mixture under loosened skin. Place chicken on a broiler pan. Insert meat thermometer into meaty part of thigh, making sure not to touch bone.

3. Remove white papery skin from garlic heads (do not peel or separate the cloves). Wrap each head separately in foil; place on broiler pan with chicken. Bake at 375° for 45 minutes. Increase oven temperature to 450° (do not remove chicken from oven). Bake 30 minutes or until thermometer registers 180°. Cover chicken loosely with foil; let stand 10 minutes. Discard skin. Yield: 2 servings (serving size: 1 leg quarter and 1 garlic head).

POINTS **value:**
7

exchanges:
5 lean meat

per serving:
Calories 297
Fat 11.9g (saturated fat 2.5g)
Protein 39.8g
Carbohydrate 5.7g
Fiber 0.8g
Cholesterol 154mg
Iron 2.6mg
Sodium 760mg
Calcium 59mg

TURKEY CUTLETS WITH BALSAMIC–BROWN SUGAR SAUCE

pictured on page 133

The sweet-acidic pungency of balsamic vinegar really makes this dish come alive.
Serve with soft polenta topped with shredded Parmesan cheese.

POINTS value:
6

exchanges:
1 starch
6 very lean meat

per serving:
Calories 281
Fat 4.4g (saturated fat 0.5g)
Protein 43.7g
Carbohydrate 15.5g
Fiber 0.6g
Cholesterol 68mg
Iron 3.3mg
Sodium 706mg
Calcium 22mg

¼ cup all-purpose flour
1 teaspoon dried thyme
½ teaspoon salt
½ teaspoon pepper
1½ pounds turkey cutlets
1 tablespoon olive oil
¼ cup minced shallots
⅔ cup dry red wine
⅔ cup fat-free, less-sodium chicken broth
¼ cup balsamic vinegar
2 tablespoons brown sugar
¼ teaspoon salt
Thyme sprigs (optional)

1. Combine first 4 ingredients in a shallow dish; stir well. Dredge turkey cutlets in flour mixture.
2. Heat oil in a large nonstick skillet over medium-high heat. Add cutlets, and cook 3 minutes on each side or until done. Remove cutlets from pan; set aside, and keep warm. Reduce heat to medium.
3. Add shallots to pan, and sauté 1 minute. Stir in wine and broth, scraping pan to loosen browned bits. Bring to a boil, and cook 5 minutes. Add vinegar, sugar, and ¼ teaspoon salt; bring to a boil. Reduce heat, and simmer 3 minutes. Serve sauce with cutlets. Garnish with thyme sprigs, if desired. Yield: 4 servings (serving size: 4 ounces turkey and 2 tablespoons sauce).

prep: 10 minutes ★ **cook:** 1 hour and 45 minutes ★ **other:** 2 hours and 10 minutes

CHILI-SPICED SMOKED TURKEY BREAST

If you love smoked turkey but don't want to drag out the smoker, this recipe is the answer. Simply place the turkey breast on the cool side of a covered gas grill and use soaked mesquite wood chips. You'll get all the smoky flavor without the fuss.

¼	cup fresh lime juice (about 2 limes)
2	tablespoons olive oil
2	teaspoons unsweetened cocoa
2	teaspoons paprika
2	teaspoons brown sugar
1	teaspoon salt
1	teaspoon dried oregano
1	teaspoon dried thyme
1	teaspoon chili powder
2	garlic cloves, minced
1	(6-pound) whole turkey breast
2	cups mesquite chips

Cooking spray

POINTS value:
3

exchanges:
3½ very lean meat

per serving:
Calories 126
Fat 1.6g (saturated fat 0.3g)
Protein 25.6g
Carbohydrate 0.6g
Fiber 0.1g
Cholesterol 71mg
Iron 1.4mg
Sodium 119mg
Calcium 13mg

1. Combine first 10 ingredients in a small saucepan; bring to a boil. Remove from heat; cool. Combine lime juice mixture and turkey breast in a large zip-top plastic bag. Seal bag, and marinate in refrigerator 2 hours. While turkey marinates, soak wood chips in water at least 30 minutes. Drain well.

2. Preheat gas grill to medium-hot (350° to 400°) using both burners. Turn left burner off. Place wood chips in a disposable foil pan or a foil packet pierced with holes on grill over right burner. Coat grill rack with cooking spray. Remove turkey from bag; discard marinade. Place turkey, skin side up, on grill rack over left burner. Cover and cook 1½ hours. Turn turkey over; cook 15 minutes or until meat thermometer registers 170°. Remove turkey from grill. Cover loosely with foil, and let stand at least 10 minutes before carving. Discard skin. Yield: 16 servings (serving size: 3 ounces).

ORANGE-BOURBON TURKEY

POINTS value:
6

exchanges:
1 starch
7 very lean meat

per serving:
Calories 305
Fat 4.1g (saturated fat 1.3g)
Protein 51g
Carbohydrate 12.8g
Fiber 0.1g
Cholesterol 142mg
Iron 3.5mg
Sodium 251mg
Calcium 54mg

1   (12-pound) fresh or frozen whole turkey, thawed
2   cups fresh orange juice (about 6 oranges)
1   cup water
¾   cup bourbon, divided
⅓   cup molasses
¾   teaspoon salt, divided
4   oranges, peeled
Cooking spray
3   tablespoons all-purpose flour

1. Remove giblets and neck from turkey; discard. Rinse turkey thoroughly under cold water; pat dry. Combine orange juice, water, ½ cup bourbon, and molasses in a 2-gallon heavy-duty zip-top plastic bag; add turkey. Seal bag, and marinate in refrigerator 4 to 24 hours, turning bag occasionally. Remove turkey from bag, reserving marinade. Return marinade to refrigerator.

2. Preheat oven to 350°.

3. Tie ends of legs with cord. Lift wing tips up and over back, and tuck under bird. Sprinkle ½ teaspoon salt into body cavity. Stuff cavity with 4 oranges. Place turkey on a broiler pan coated with cooking spray or on a rack set in a shallow roasting pan. Insert meat thermometer into meaty part of thigh, making sure not to touch bone. Bake at 350° for 3 hours or until thermometer registers 180°. (Cover turkey loosely with foil if it gets too brown.) Remove turkey from oven. Cover turkey loosely with foil; let stand at least 10 minutes before carving. Discard oranges.

4. While turkey stands, pour reserved marinade into a saucepan; bring to a boil. Skim foam from mixture with a slotted spoon; discard. Reduce heat to medium; cook until reduced to 3½ cups (about 15 minutes). Combine ¼ cup bourbon and flour in a small bowl, stirring well with a whisk. Add to reduced marinade; bring to a boil, and cook 1 minute, stirring constantly. Stir in ¼ teaspoon salt. Serve sauce with turkey. Yield: 12 servings (serving size: 6 ounces turkey and ¼ cup sauce).

Turkey Cutlets with Balsamic-Brown Sugar Sauce, page 130

Roasted Lemon Chicken with Potatoes,
page 128

Oven-Fried Chicken, page 126

Collard Greens with Lima Beans
and Smoked Turkey

prep: 10 minutes ★ **cook:** 2 hours and 45 minutes

COLLARD GREENS WITH LIMA BEANS AND SMOKED TURKEY

pictured on facing page

Nutritious, flavor-packed winter greens steal the show in this one-pot meal. It can be made up to three days ahead and refrigerated.

1½	cups dried baby lima beans
1	tablespoon olive oil
2	cups vertically sliced red onion
3	cups fat-free, less-sodium chicken broth
1	cup diced smoked turkey breast (about 6 ounces)
½	teaspoon dried thyme
¼	teaspoon crushed red pepper
3	garlic cloves, minced
1	bay leaf
8	cups sliced collard greens (about ½ pound)
2	tablespoons red wine vinegar
1	(14.5-ounce) can diced tomatoes, undrained
¼	teaspoon salt
¼	teaspoon black pepper
Thyme sprigs (optional)	

***POINTS* value:**
4

exchanges:
2 starch
2 very lean meat

per serving:
Calories 230
Fat 3.3g (saturated fat 0.7g)
Protein 17.4g
Carbohydrate 34.5g
Fiber 18.3g
Cholesterol 14mg
Iron 3.5mg
Sodium 604mg
Calcium 216mg

1. Sort and wash beans; place in a large ovenproof Dutch oven. Cover with water to 2 inches above beans; bring to a boil, and cook 20 minutes. Remove from heat; drain beans in a colander. Wipe pan dry with a paper towel.
2. Preheat oven to 375°.
3. Heat oil in pan over medium-low heat. Add onion; sauté 10 minutes. Add beans, broth, and next 5 ingredients; bring to a boil. Cover and bake at 375° for 1 hour and 15 minutes. Stir in collards, vinegar, and tomatoes. Cover and bake 1 hour or until beans are tender, stirring occasionally. Stir in salt and pepper. Discard bay leaf. Garnish with thyme sprigs, if desired. Yield: 7 servings (serving size: 1 cup).

SAUSAGE, GARLIC, AND MUSHROOM PIZZA

With lots of garlic and two kinds of pungent cheese, this pizza really delivers a punch of flavor.

POINTS value:
6

exchanges:
1½ starch
2 medium-fat meat

per serving:
Calories 267
Fat 10.1g (saturated fat 4.3g)
Protein 18.2g
Carbohydrate 26g
Fiber 1.4g
Cholesterol 44mg
Iron 2.2mg
Sodium 625mg
Calcium 272mg

8   ounces turkey Italian sausage
Cooking spray
4   cups finely chopped mushrooms (about 12 ounces)
½   cup diced onion
6   garlic cloves, minced
¼   cup evaporated fat-free milk
3   tablespoons chopped fresh parsley
½   cup (2 ounces) shredded provolone cheese
1   (10-ounce) Italian cheese-flavored thin pizza crust
     (such as Boboli)
¼   cup grated fresh Romano cheese

1. Preheat oven to 450°.
2. Remove sausage from casings. Cook sausage in a large nonstick skillet over medium-high heat until browned, stirring to crumble. Drain. Wipe drippings from pan with a paper towel.
3. Coat pan with cooking spray; place over medium-high heat. Add mushrooms, onion, and garlic; sauté 7 minutes or until liquid evaporates. Add milk and parsley. Cook mixture 2 minutes.
4. Sprinkle provolone cheese over crust, leaving a ½-inch border. Spread mushroom mixture evenly over cheese, and top with turkey sausage. Sprinkle Romano cheese over pizza. Bake on center rack of oven at 450° for 8 to 10 minutes. Remove to a cutting board; cut into 6 wedges. Serve immediately. Yield: 6 servings (serving size: 1 slice).

Salads

CREAMY CAESAR SALAD WITH SPICY CROUTONS

Creamy dressing, crunchy croutons, and characteristic Mediterranean ingredients make this salad one of our all-time favorites.

POINTS value:
2

exchanges:
1 starch
1 vegetable
½ fat

per serving:
Calories 137
Fat 4.1g (saturated fat 1.3g)
Protein 7.7g
Carbohydrate 18.2g
Fiber 4.1g
Cholesterol 4mg
Iron 3mg
Sodium 836mg
Calcium 176mg

1	garlic clove, peeled and halved
½	cup fat-free mayonnaise
2	tablespoons red wine vinegar
2	teaspoons Dijon mustard
2	teaspoons white wine Worcestershire sauce
1	teaspoon anchovy paste (optional)
¼	teaspoon pepper
2	teaspoons olive oil
¾	teaspoon Cajun seasoning
1	garlic clove, minced
2	cups (¾-inch) cubed sourdough bread
18	cups torn romaine lettuce
⅓	cup (1⅓ ounces) grated fresh Parmesan cheese

1. Drop garlic halves through opening in blender lid with blender on; process until minced. Add mayonnaise and next 5 ingredients; process until well blended. Cover and chill at least 1 hour.

2. Preheat oven to 400°.

3. Combine oil, Cajun seasoning, and minced garlic in a medium microwave-safe bowl. Microwave at HIGH 20 seconds. Add bread cubes; toss gently to coat. Spread bread cubes in a single layer on a baking sheet; bake at 400° for 15 minutes or until golden brown.

4. Place lettuce in a large bowl. Add dressing; toss gently to coat. Sprinkle with cheese, and top with croutons. Yield: 6 servings (serving size: 2 cups).

SPRING SALAD WITH ASPARAGUS AND RADISHES

Whether they're thick or thin, use asparagus stalks of approximately the same size so that they cook evenly.

1	cup (1-inch) diagonally sliced asparagus (about 6 ounces)
3	cups gourmet salad greens
3	radishes, thinly sliced
1½	tablespoons fat-free red wine vinaigrette (such as Girard's)
½	teaspoon country-style Dijon mustard
1½	tablespoons (about ½ ounce) finely crumbled feta cheese

1. Steam asparagus, covered, 3 minutes or until tender. Rinse asparagus under cold water, and pat dry. Combine steamed asparagus, greens, and radishes in a large bowl. Combine vinaigrette and mustard in a small bowl; stir well with a whisk. Add vinaigrette mixture and crumbled feta to salad, tossing gently to coat. Yield: 2 servings (serving size: 1½ cups).

Note: You can prepare the greens, asparagus, and radishes up to 1 hour ahead. Combine them in a large bowl, cover with a paper towel, and chill.

POINTS value:
1

exchanges:
2 vegetable

per serving:
Calories 58
Fat 1.9g (saturated fat 1.1g)
Protein 3.9g
Carbohydrate 7.6g
Fiber 2.9g
Cholesterol 6mg
Iron 1.6mg
Sodium 348mg
Calcium 81mg

Asparagus: When selecting asparagus, reach for green instead of white: The green variety is higher in vitamins A and C and in folate. Choose asparagus spears with tight, compact tips and a similar diameter so they'll all cook at the same rate. As for cooking asparagus, the secret is simple: Don't overcook it. The slender shoots should turn out crisp and bright in color. And while you might want to snip the woody ends of the shoots before cooking, there's no reason to toss them away. You can make a fantastic asparagus soup out of those ends.

prep: 13 minutes ★ cook: 2 minutes ★ other: 3 hours

ASPARAGUS–APPLE SALAD

Fresh asparagus, crisp, juicy apples, and sweet raisins are so flavorful that this salad needs nothing more than a drizzle of dill vinaigrette. It can be made up to 12 hours before it's served. The longer it marinates, the more flavorful it becomes.

POINTS value:
2

exchanges:
½ starch
½ fruit
1 vegetable

per serving:
Calories 99
Fat 2.3g (saturated fat 0.3g)
Protein 1.7g
Carbohydrate 20.5g
Fiber 2.9g
Cholesterol 0mg
Iron 0.8mg
Sodium 88mg
Calcium 23mg

3 cups (1-inch) diagonally sliced asparagus (about 1 pound)
4 cups cubed Red Delicious apple (about 1¼ pounds)
2 teaspoons fresh lemon juice
¼ cup raisins
2 tablespoons cider vinegar
1 tablespoon olive oil
2 teaspoons honey
¼ teaspoon salt
¼ teaspoon dried dill
⅛ teaspoon pepper
7 curly leaf lettuce leaves

1. Steam asparagus, covered, 2 minutes or until crisp-tender. Rinse asparagus under cold water, and pat dry.
2. Combine apple and lemon juice in a large bowl, tossing well to coat. Add asparagus and raisins, tossing gently.
3. Combine cider vinegar and next 5 ingredients; stir well with a whisk. Pour vinaigrette over salad; toss gently to coat. Cover and chill 3 to 12 hours. Serve on lettuce leaves. Yield: 7 servings (serving size: 1 cup).

prep: 12 minutes ★ **cook:** 16 minutes

MESCLUN WITH CARAMELIZED ONION, APPLE, AND GRUYÈRE CHEESE

Thin slices of onion—sprinkled with sugar and cooked until golden—perfectly complement the nutty cheese and sweet apple in this salad of mixed baby greens.

Cooking spray
8   (¼-inch-thick) slices onion
1   teaspoon sugar, divided
6   cups gourmet salad greens
1   cup sliced Fuji or Gala apple
¼   cup (1 ounce) grated Gruyère cheese
1   tablespoon water
1   tablespoon white wine vinegar
1   teaspoon olive oil
¼   teaspoon salt
¼   teaspoon pepper

POINTS value:
2

exchanges:
2½ vegetable
½ fat

per serving:
Calories 86
Fat 3.9g (saturated fat 1.5g)
Protein 3.9g
Carbohydrate 9.8g
Fiber 2.8g
Cholesterol 8mg
Iron 1.1mg
Sodium 178mg
Calcium 110mg

1. Place a large nonstick skillet coated with cooking spray
over medium heat. Arrange 4 onion slices in pan, and sprinkle with ½ teaspoon sugar; cook 4 minutes on each side or
until golden brown. Wipe pan clean with paper towels;
repeat procedure with remaining onion slices and ½ teaspoon sugar.
2. Combine salad greens, apple, and cheese. Combine
water, vinegar, oil, salt, and pepper; pour vinaigrette over
salad, tossing to coat. Place salad on each of 4 plates; top each
with onion slices. Yield: 4 servings (serving size: 1½ cups
salad and 2 onion slices).

SPINACH-STRAWBERRY SALAD WITH GOAT-CHEESE BRUSCHETTA

POINTS value:
4

exchanges:
1 starch
1 fruit
1 vegetable
1 fat

per serving:
Calories 213
Fat 6.7g (saturated fat 2.7g)
Protein 7.1g
Carbohydrate 31g
Fiber 4.5g
Cholesterol 13mg
Iron 2.7mg
Sodium 446mg
Calcium 163mg

¼ cup sugar
2 tablespoons sherry vinegar or white wine vinegar
1½ teaspoons sesame seeds, toasted
1 teaspoon minced red onion
1½ teaspoons olive oil
¾ teaspoon poppy seeds
¼ teaspoon Hungarian sweet paprika
⅛ teaspoon salt
6 cups torn spinach (about 1 pound)
2 cups halved strawberries
2 tablespoons slivered almonds, toasted
1 (3-ounce) log goat cheese, cut into 6 slices
6 (1-ounce) slices French bread, toasted

1. Combine first 8 ingredients in a jar; cover tightly, and shake vigorously.

2. Combine spinach and strawberry halves in a large bowl, and toss gently. Pour vinaigrette over salad, tossing gently to coat. Place 1 cup salad on each of 6 plates; sprinkle each serving with 1 teaspoon toasted almonds. Spread cheese over toast slices; top each salad with 1 bruschetta. Yield: 6 servings.

Super Spinach: Spinach contains vitamins and minerals as well as high levels of lutein—a phytochemical that protects the eyes from harmful ultraviolet rays.

TUSCAN BREAD SALAD WITH CORN

1	cup fresh corn kernels (about 2 ears)
½	cup water
2	cups (1-inch) cubed Italian bread
3	garlic cloves, minced
2	tablespoons white wine vinegar
2	tablespoons water
2	tablespoons mango chutney
1	tablespoon olive oil
¼	teaspoon salt
¼	teaspoon coarsely ground black pepper
1	cup chopped seeded peeled cucumber
1	cup chopped seeded tomato
½	cup chopped green onions
½	cup chopped yellow bell pepper

POINTS value:
2

exchanges:
1 starch
1 vegetable
½ fat

per serving:
Calories 116
Fat 2.9g (saturated fat 0.4g)
Protein 3g
Carbohydrate 20.8g
Fiber 2.2g
Cholesterol 0mg
Iron 1.1mg
Sodium 207mg
Calcium 20mg

1. Preheat broiler.

2. Combine corn and ½ cup water in a small saucepan, and bring to a boil. Reduce heat, and simmer 10 minutes or until corn is tender. Drain well.

3. While corn cooks, combine bread cubes and garlic in a medium bowl; toss well to coat. Arrange bread cubes on a jelly-roll pan, and broil 5 minutes or until lightly browned, stirring once.

4. Combine vinegar and next 5 ingredients in a large bowl. Add corn, cucumber, and next 3 ingredients. Add bread cubes, and toss gently. Serve immediately. Yield: 6 servings (serving size: ¾ cup).

WHITE BEAN AND TOMATO SALAD

POINTS value:
3

exchanges:
1 starch
1 vegetable
1 fat

per serving:
Calories 142
Fat 5.6g (saturated fat 1.7g)
Protein 6.1g
Carbohydrate 16.4g
Fiber 2.8g
Cholesterol 7mg
Iron 1.5mg
Sodium 512mg
Calcium 77mg

2   (15-ounce) cans cannellini beans or Great Northern beans, rinsed and drained
1½ cups chopped tomato
⅓   cup thinly sliced fresh basil
⅓   cup (1⅓ ounces) crumbled feta cheese
¼   cup white balsamic vinegar
½   teaspoon sugar
1½ tablespoons olive oil
¼   teaspoon salt
¼   teaspoon freshly ground black pepper

1. Combine first 4 ingredients in a bowl; set aside.
2. Combine vinegar and next 4 ingredients in a small jar. Cover tightly, and shake vigorously. Pour vinaigrette over bean mixture. Let stand at room temperature 30 minutes, stirring occasionally. Yield: 6 servings (serving size: ¾ cup).

Best Winter Picks: Some tomatoes are better than others in winter. Best bets are vine-ripened, Roma, and cherry tomatoes. Vine-ripened tomatoes are small to medium in size and are often sold in clusters still attached to a vine. Oval Roma, or plum, tomatoes have firmer pulp and fewer seeds than other varieties, so they hold their shape well. Cherry and grape tomatoes are always flavorful because their size, shape, and packaging protects them.

ORIENTAL PASTA SALAD

Dark sesame oil gives this side salad a distinct flavor. Serve it with
grilled teriyaki chicken or pork.

3	ounces uncooked spaghetti
2	cups broccoli florets
¾	cup thinly sliced red bell pepper
2	tablespoons low-sodium soy sauce
1	tablespoon dark sesame oil

1. Cook pasta according to package directions, omitting
salt and fat.
2. While pasta cooks, steam broccoli, covered, 5 minutes or
until crisp-tender. Rinse under cold water; drain well.
3. Combine pasta, broccoli, and remaining ingredients; toss
gently. Cover and chill 1 hour. Yield: 4 servings (serving
size: 1 cup).

Sesame Oil isn't as high in monounsaturated fat as olive
oil, but it's high in polyunsaturated fat, ranking fourth behind
safflower, soybean, and corn oil. Light sesame oil (light in
color, not in fat) has a deliciously delicate, nutty flavor and is
good for everything from sautéing to salad dressings. Dark
sesame oil has a much stronger flavor and fragrance and
is often used to add a distinct accent to a dish.

POINTS value:
3

exchanges:
1 starch
1 vegetable
½ fat

per serving:
Calories 131
Fat 4g (saturated fat 0.6g)
Protein 4.5g
Carbohydrate 20g
Fiber 2.2g
Cholesterol 0mg
Iron 1.7mg
Sodium 255mg
Calcium 26mg

GERMAN HOT POTATO SALAD

Turkey bacon, cider vinegar, lots of onions, and a spoonful of sugar star in this traditionally high-fat salad. You'll never miss the fat and calories in this healthful recipe, and we bet you'll give it an A+ for flavor.

POINTS value:
3

exchanges:
1½ starch
½ fat

per serving:
Calories 144
Fat 2.1g (saturated fat 0.5g)
Protein 6.5g
Carbohydrate 25g
Fiber 2.5g
Cholesterol 9mg
Iron 2mg
Sodium 388mg
Calcium 25mg

8 cups (¼-inch-thick) sliced red potato (about 2 pounds)
2 tablespoons minced fresh parsley
½ teaspoon celery seeds
Cooking spray
4 slices turkey bacon, minced
1 cup chopped onion
2½ tablespoons all-purpose flour
⅓ cup plus 1 tablespoon cider vinegar
1 tablespoon sugar
¼ teaspoon pepper
1 (10½-ounce) can beef broth

1. Place potato in a Dutch oven; cover with water, and bring to a boil. Cook 8 minutes or until tender. Drain and place in a large bowl. Sprinkle with parsley and celery seeds; set aside.
2. Heat a medium nonstick skillet coated with cooking spray over medium-high heat. Add bacon, and sauté 3 minutes or until crisp. Add onion, and sauté 3 minutes or until tender. Add bacon and onion to potato mixture.
3. Place flour in a small bowl. Gradually add cider vinegar, stirring well with a whisk.
4. Combine sugar, pepper, and broth in pan. Bring to a boil, and cook 2 minutes. Add flour mixture to pan, and cook 3 minutes or until thick (mixture will reduce to about 1 cup). Pour over potato mixture, and toss gently to coat. Serve warm. Yield: 8 servings (serving size: 1 cup).

FIERY THAI BEEF SALAD

pictured on page 153

The fresh lime juice, cilantro, chiles, and fish sauce create a tart, spicy dressing for this main-dish salad that earned top ratings from our test kitchen.

⅓	cup fresh lime juice
¼	cup chopped fresh cilantro
2	tablespoons brown sugar
1	tablespoon water
1	tablespoon Thai fish sauce
5	garlic cloves, minced
2	Thai, hot red, or serrano chiles, seeded and minced
1	(1-pound) flank steak, trimmed
¼	teaspoon salt
⅛	teaspoon black pepper
Cooking spray	
6	cups torn romaine lettuce
1¾	cups quartered cherry tomatoes
1	cup thinly sliced red onion, separated into rings
¼	cup coarsely chopped fresh mint
2	tablespoons sliced peeled fresh lemon grass

POINTS value:
6

exchanges:
½ starch
2 vegetable
3 lean meat

per serving:
Calories 265
Fat 11.3g (saturated fat 4.7g)
Protein 25.5g
Carbohydrate 16g
Fiber 3g
Cholesterol 57mg
Iron 4.1mg
Sodium 572mg
Calcium 65mg

1. Combine first 7 ingredients in a bowl; stir well with a whisk.
2. Prepare grill or broiler.
3. Sprinkle both sides of steak with salt and pepper. Place steak on grill rack or broiler pan coated with cooking spray, and cook 6 minutes on each side or until desired degree of doneness. Let stand 10 minutes. Cut steak diagonally across grain into thin slices; cut each slice into 2-inch pieces.
4. Combine steak, lettuce, and next 4 ingredients in a large bowl; add dressing, tossing to coat. Yield: 4 servings (serving size: 2 cups).

TABBOULEH WITH ARUGULA AND CHICKEN

pictured on page 154

Paired with pita bread, this no-cook main-dish salad is ideal for brown
bag lunches or a light springtime supper. You'll find bulgur in
most supermarkets next to the pasta and rice.

POINTS value:
4

exchanges:
1½ starch
1 vegetable
2 very lean meat

per serving:
Calories 218
Fat 5g (saturated fat 0.9g)
Protein 14.9g
Carbohydrate 31g
Fiber 7.5g
Cholesterol 26mg
Iron 1.5mg
Sodium 379mg
Calcium 43mg

1 cup uncooked bulgur
1 cup boiling water
1½ cups chopped ready-to-eat roasted skinless, boneless chicken breasts (about 2 breasts)
1 cup diced tomato
½ cup chopped arugula or spinach (about ½ ounce)
⅓ cup diced red onion
¼ cup finely chopped fresh parsley
2 tablespoons finely chopped fresh mint
2 tablespoons fresh lemon juice
1 tablespoon olive oil
¼ teaspoon salt
⅛ teaspoon pepper
Arugula or spinach leaves (optional)

1. Combine bulgur and boiling water in a large bowl.
Cover and let stand 25 minutes. Stir in chicken and next 9
ingredients; cover and chill. Garnish with arugula leaves, if
desired. Yield: 4 servings (serving size: 1½ cups).

Side Dishes

Stovetop "Baked Beans"

We took baked beans out of the oven and put them onto the stovetop so they're ready in half the time it takes to cook traditional slow-baked beans. Maple syrup and brown sugar add sweetness while barbecue seasoning adds smokiness—a combination the whole family is sure to love.

POINTS value:
3

exchanges:
2½ starch

per serving:
Calories 179
Fat 2.1g (saturated fat 0.9g)
Protein 5.1g
Carbohydrate 37.1g
Fiber 4.2g
Cholesterol 3.8mg
Iron 1.8mg
Sodium 467mg
Calcium 64.5mg

1   tablespoon butter
1¼   cups chopped onion
¾   cup chopped green bell pepper
2   garlic cloves, minced
1   cup ketchup
¼   cup packed brown sugar
¼   cup maple syrup
2   tablespoons Worcestershire sauce
2   teaspoons barbecue smoke seasoning (such as Hickory Liquid Smoke)
2   teaspoons prepared mustard
1   (16-ounce) can red beans, rinsed and drained
1   (15.8-ounce) can Great Northern beans, rinsed and drained

1. Melt butter in a medium saucepan over medium-high heat. Add onion, bell pepper, and garlic; sauté 4 minutes. Stir in ketchup and remaining ingredients; bring to a boil. Reduce heat; simmer 15 minutes, stirring occasionally. Yield: 8 servings (serving size: ½ cup).

Fiery Thai Beef Salad, page 149

**Tabbouleh with Arugula and Chicken,
page 150**

Squash-Rice Casserole, page 160

Summer Vegetable Stew with Basil Purée,
page 188

ROASTED CAULIFLOWER

Mellow, slightly sweet roasted garlic and onions round out the flavor
of golden-roasted cauliflower.

2   teaspoons olive oil
2   medium onions, quartered
5   garlic cloves, halved
4   cups cauliflower florets (about 1½ pounds)
Cooking spray
1   tablespoon water
1   tablespoon Dijon mustard
½   teaspoon salt
¼   teaspoon freshly ground black pepper
1   tablespoon chopped fresh flat-leaf parsley

1. Preheat oven to 500°.

2. Heat oil in a large skillet over medium heat. Add onions
and garlic; cook 5 minutes or until browned, stirring frequently. Remove from heat.

3. Place onion mixture and cauliflower in a roasting pan
coated with cooking spray. Combine water and mustard;
pour over vegetable mixture. Sprinkle with salt and pepper;
toss to coat. Bake at 500° for 20 minutes or until golden
brown, stirring occasionally. Sprinkle with parsley. Yield: 4
servings (serving size: 1 cup).

POINTS value:
1

exchanges:
3 vegetable
½ fat

per serving:
Calories 94
Fat 3.1g (saturated fat 0.4g)
Protein 4.5g
Carbohydrate 15.4g
Fiber 5.4g
Cholesterol 0mg
Iron 1.1mg
Sodium 408mg
Calcium 63mg

GREEN BEANS NIÇOISE

Ideal for entertaining, the green beans and the tomato mixture can be prepared a day in advance; cover and chill them separately. To coat the beans evenly with the dressing, toss them before serving.

POINTS value:
1

exchanges:
2 vegetable
½ fat

per serving:
Calories 68
Fat 2.2g (saturated fat 0.3g)
Protein 2.6g
Carbohydrate 11.5g
Fiber 2.8g
Cholesterol 0mg
Iron 1.5mg
Sodium 213mg
Calcium 49mg

2   pounds green beans, trimmed
1⅓ cups chopped plum tomato (about ¾ pound)
½   cup minced shallots
¼   cup water
2   tablespoons chopped ripe olives
2   tablespoons red wine vinegar
1   tablespoon olive oil
2   teaspoons Dijon mustard
½   teaspoon salt

1. Cook beans in boiling water 5 minutes or until crisp-tender. Drain and plunge beans into ice water; drain. Place beans in a large bowl.
2. Combine tomato and next 7 ingredients; pour over beans, and toss gently. Yield: 8 servings (serving size: 1 cup).

Shallots: Because of their low water content, shallots have a more concentrated flavor than onions. They can also burn and toughen easily, so use caution when sautéing. When peeling a shallot, remove a couple of the outer layers along with the peel. You might need an extra shallot to make up for the discarded layers, but this method is a lot faster than removing only the thin peel.

CREAMED SPINACH

You'll never miss the fat in this classic side thanks to the light cream cheese
that provides a smooth, rich sauce for the spinach.

2   (10-ounce) packages fresh spinach
Cooking spray
2   tablespoons minced shallots
2   teaspoons all-purpose flour
⅛   teaspoon salt
⅛   teaspoon ground nutmeg
½   cup fat-free milk
½   cup tub-style light cream cheese, softened

1. Remove large stems from spinach. Rinse spinach under
cold water; drain. Place a large Dutch oven over medium
heat, and add spinach. (Spinach will need to be tightly
packed into the pan to cook all of it in one batch.) Cover
and cook 5 minutes or until spinach wilts, stirring well
after 2 minutes. Place spinach in a colander, and drain well,
pressing spinach with the back of a spoon to remove as
much moisture as possible.
2. Heat pan coated with cooking spray over medium heat.
Add shallots; sauté 2 minutes. Combine flour, salt, and nutmeg; add to pan, stirring well. Cook 30 seconds. Add milk
and cheese, stirring with a whisk; cook 1 minute or until
thick, stirring constantly. Add spinach; cook 1 minute or
until thoroughly heated. Serve immediately. Yield: 4 servings (serving size: ⅔ cup).

***POINTS* value:**
2

exchanges:
2 vegetable
1 very lean meat
½ fat

per serving:
Calories 110
Fat 5.4g (saturated fat 3g)
Protein 8g
Carbohydrate 9.4g
Fiber 5.4g
Cholesterol 17mg
Iron 3.8mg
Sodium 354mg
Calcium 210mg

SESAME SUGAR SNAP PEAS

Create an exciting Asian menu when you serve these peas with teriyaki pork, beef, or chicken and a side of Chinese-style noodles.

POINTS value:
1

exchanges:
2 vegetable
½ fat

per serving:
Calories 81
Fat 1.1g (saturated fat 0.2g)
Protein 2.8g
Carbohydrate 16g
Fiber 3.6g
Cholesterol 0mg
Iron 1.4mg
Sodium 369mg
Calcium 51mg

Cooking spray
1   teaspoon dark sesame oil
2   (8-ounce) packages frozen sugar snap peas
1   (8-ounce) can sliced water chestnuts, drained
¼   cup low-sodium soy sauce
3   tablespoons brown sugar
1   tablespoon minced peeled fresh ginger
2   teaspoons cornstarch

1. Coat a large nonstick skillet with cooking spray; add oil. Place over medium-high heat until hot. Add peas and water chestnuts; sauté 4 minutes or until peas are crisp-tender.
2. Combine soy sauce and remaining 3 ingredients, stirring until smooth. Add to vegetable mixture. Bring to a boil, and cook 2 minutes or until thick and bubbly, stirring constantly. Yield: 6 servings (serving size: ¾ cup).

Ginger: Look for fresh ginger in the produce section of your supermarket. Choose the freshest, youngest-looking gingerroot you can find. Old roots are fibrous, tough, and flavorless.

Store fresh unpeeled ginger tightly wrapped in plastic wrap in the vegetable crisper section of the refrigerator up to 3 weeks. Or store whole fresh unpeeled ginger in a jar of sherry in the refrigerator, and use both the ginger and the sherry in Asian dishes.

GRILLED MARINATED VEGETABLES

Trumpet the year's new crop of vegetables with this colorful, easy-to-make side dish. While you're grilling the veggies, add some chicken breasts or salmon fillets to the grill, and dinner is done with very little to clean up afterwards.

¾   pound small red potatoes, cut into ½-inch pieces
1   cup (½-inch-thick) sliced yellow squash
1   cup (½-inch-thick) sliced zucchini
1   small onion, cut into 8 wedges
1   large red bell pepper, cut into ½-inch-wide strips
⅓   cup rice vinegar
1   tablespoon fresh lemon juice
1   tablespoon Dijon mustard
1½   teaspoons dark sesame oil
⅛   teaspoon salt
⅛   teaspoon black pepper
2   garlic cloves, minced
Cooking spray

POINTS value:
2

exchanges:
½ starch
1½ vegetable

per serving:
Calories 99
Fat 2.1g (saturated fat 0.3g)
Protein 2.8g
Carbohydrate 18.1g
Fiber 2.9g
Cholesterol 0mg
Iron 1.7mg
Sodium 158mg
Calcium 27mg

1. Place potato in a medium saucepan; cover with water, and bring to a boil. Reduce heat, and simmer, uncovered, 10 to 12 minutes or until tender; drain.
2. Combine potato, yellow squash, and next 10 ingredients in a large zip-top plastic bag. Seal bag, and marinate 30 minutes at room temperature, turning bag occasionally.
3. Prepare grill.
4. Remove vegetables from bag, reserving marinade. Place vegetables in a wire grilling basket coated with cooking spray. Place grilling basket on grill rack, and grill 8 minutes on each side or until tender. Place vegetables in a bowl. Pour reserved marinade over vegetables; toss gently. Yield: 5 servings (serving size: 1 cup).

SMASHED POTATO-AND-BROCCOLI CASSEROLE

Feed a crowd and simplify the dinner hour with this cheesy casserole. You can put the casserole together earlier in the day; then as it bakes, you'll have time to relax. Increase the serving size to 1 cup for a meatless main dish with a **POINTS** value of 6.

POINTS value:
4

exchanges:
2 starch
1 vegetable
1 fat

per serving:
Calories 219
Fat 4.2g (saturated fat 2.4g)
Protein 11.2g
Carbohydrate 34.1g
Fiber 2.9g
Cholesterol 14.3mg
Iron 1.9mg
Sodium 304mg
Calcium 193mg

2   pounds baking potatoes, halved
1   cup chopped broccoli
½   cup diced onion
½   cup part-skim ricotta cheese
1½ teaspoons chopped fresh or ½ teaspoon dried dill
½   teaspoon salt
⅛   teaspoon ground red pepper
1   (8-ounce) container fat-free sour cream
Cooking spray
¾   cup (3 ounces) shredded reduced-fat sharp Cheddar cheese

1. Preheat oven to 375°.
2. Place potatoes in a saucepan; cover with water. Bring to a boil. Reduce heat; simmer 20 minutes or until tender. Drain potatoes in a colander over a bowl, reserving 1 cup cooking liquid. Return potatoes and reserved liquid to pan; mash with a potato masher until slightly chunky.
3. Add broccoli and next 6 ingredients to pan, and stir well. Spoon potato mixture into an 11 x 7-inch baking dish coated with cooking spray; bake at 375° for 35 minutes. Sprinkle with Cheddar cheese; bake an additional 5 minutes or until cheese melts. Yield: 8 servings (serving size: ¾ cup).

prep: 15 minutes ★ **cook:** 25 minutes

FETA MASHED POTATOES

Serve these spuds with Greek-seasoned chicken breasts and a salad for
a quick-and-easy meal fit for company.

2	pounds baking potatoes, peeled and cubed (about 5¼ cups)
¼	cup fat-free milk
3	tablespoons (¾ ounce) crumbled feta cheese
2	tablespoons fat-free sour cream
½	teaspoon salt
½	teaspoon dried oregano
¼	teaspoon pepper

1. Place potato in a large saucepan, and cover with water; bring to a boil. Cover potatoes, reduce heat, and simmer 20 minutes or until potato is very tender.

2. Drain potato well, and return to pan; beat with a mixer at high speed until smooth. Add remaining ingredients, and beat well. Yield: 8 servings (serving size: ½ cup).

POINTS **value:**
2

exchanges:
1 starch

per serving:
Calories 94
Fat 0.9g (saturated fat 0.6g)
Protein 3.1g
Carbohydrate 18.7g
Fiber 1.6g
Cholesterol 3mg
Iron 0.8mg
Sodium 200mg
Calcium 37mg

Tips for Marvelous Mashed Potatoes:

•Cube the potatoes before cooking. Although you can cook them whole, it takes longer.

•After you drain the potatoes, place the pan over low heat, then shake the potatoes in the pan to dry them before mashing. If your pan is stainless, mash the potatoes right in the pan over low heat to keep them warm.

•To reduce the potential for lumps, warm the milk before you mash it with the potatoes.

GRILLED SWEET POTATOES WITH ORANGE-CHIPOTLE GLAZE

Sweet potatoes stand up to bold, spicy glazes and pair perfectly with grilled chicken.

POINTS value:
3

exchanges:
2 starch
½ fat

per serving:
Calories 185
Fat 3.5g (saturated fat 1.9g)
Protein 2.4g
Carbohydrate 36.6g
Fiber 3.6g
Cholesterol 8mg
Iron 0.8mg
Sodium 240mg
Calcium 37mg

4 large sweet potatoes (about 2 pounds), peeled and halved lengthwise
1 (7-ounce) can chipotle chiles in adobo sauce
1 tablespoon chopped fresh cilantro
2 tablespoons butter, melted
½ teaspoon salt
1 (6-ounce) can thawed orange juice concentrate, undiluted
Cooking spray

1. Prepare grill.
2. Cook potato halves in boiling water 5 minutes or until crisp-tender; drain. Rinse under cold water; drain well.
3. While potatoes drain, remove 3 tablespoons adobo sauce from canned chiles. Place remaining sauce and chiles in a zip-top plastic bag; reserve for another use. Combine 3 tablespoons adobo sauce, cilantro, butter, salt, and orange juice concentrate in a small bowl; stir well.
4. Place potatoes on grill rack coated with cooking spray; grill 4 minutes on each side or until potatoes are done, basting frequently with orange juice mixture. Yield: 8 servings (serving size: 1 potato half).

PORTOBELLO MUSHROOM BARLEY

1   small leek (about ¼ pound)
Olive oil-flavored cooking spray
1   teaspoon olive oil
5   ounces fresh portobello mushrooms, chopped
1   garlic clove, minced
1   cup uncooked quick-cooking barley
1⅔ cups less-sodium beef broth
⅓   cup dry white wine
⅛   teaspoon salt
2   tablespoons grated Parmesan cheese

POINTS value:
3

exchanges:
2 starch
1 vegetable

per serving:
Calories 171
Fat 2.4g (saturated fat 0.7g)
Protein 7g
Carbohydrate 32g
Fiber 7.1g
Cholesterol 2mg
Iron 2mg
Sodium 247mg
Calcium 49mg

1. Remove roots, tough outer leaves, and top from leek, leaving 1½ to 2 inches of dark leaves. Finely chop leek.
2. Coat a large nonstick skillet with cooking spray; add oil. Place over medium heat until hot. Add chopped leek, mushrooms, and garlic; sauté 8 minutes or until tender. Add barley and next 3 ingredients; bring to a boil. Cover, reduce heat, and simmer 16 minutes or until barley is tender and most of liquid is absorbed. Remove from heat; let stand 5 minutes. Sprinkle with cheese, and serve immediately. Yield: 5 servings (serving size: ¾ cup).

Portobello Mushrooms: Let a cremini mushroom grow a few days longer, and you end up with a portobello. These mushrooms measure 3 to 6 inches across, and they're firm, meaty, and intensely flavorful. Before sautéing, remove the black gills on the underside of the cap to prevent the mushrooms from blackening.

SQUASH-RICE CASSEROLE
pictured on page 155

This recipe reduces your time in the kitchen because you don't have to make two sides—the rice and green vegetable are together in one creamy dish.

POINTS value:
4

exchanges:
1 starch
2 vegetable
1 medium-fat meat

per serving:
Calories 197
Fat 5.5g (saturated fat 2.7g)
Protein 12.7g
Carbohydrate 24g
Fiber 1.4g
Cholesterol 65mg
Iron 1.5mg
Sodium 623mg
Calcium 209mg

8 cups sliced zucchini (about 2½ pounds)
1 cup chopped onion
½ cup fat-free, less-sodium chicken broth
2 cups cooked rice
1 cup fat-free sour cream
1 cup (4 ounces) shredded reduced-fat sharp Cheddar cheese
¼ cup (1 ounce) grated fresh Parmesan cheese, divided
¼ cup Italian-seasoned breadcrumbs
1 teaspoon salt
¼ teaspoon pepper
2 large eggs, lightly beaten
Cooking spray

1. Preheat oven to 350°.
2. Combine first 3 ingredients in a Dutch oven; bring to a boil. Cover, reduce heat, and simmer 20 minutes or until tender. Drain; partially mash with a potato masher. Combine zucchini mixture, rice, sour cream, Cheddar cheese, 2 tablespoons Parmesan cheese, breadcrumbs, salt, pepper, and eggs in a bowl; stir gently. Spoon zucchini mixture into a 13 x 9-inch baking dish coated with cooking spray; sprinkle with 2 tablespoons Parmesan cheese. Bake at 350° for 30 minutes or until bubbly.
3. Preheat broiler.
4. Broil 1 minute or until lightly browned. Yield: 8 servings (serving size: 1 cup).

Sandwiches
&
Soups

Cucumber–Shrimp Sandwiches

You can taste summer in this sandwich of crisp cucumber and radish, fresh dill, and boiled shrimp. The only way to improve this meal is to dine poolside or beachfront.

POINTS value:
5

exchanges:
2 starch
2 very lean meat
1 fat

per serving:
Calories 261
Fat 6.6g (saturated fat 1.7g)
Protein 18g
Carbohydrate 31.8g
Fiber 4.4g
Cholesterol 93mg
Iron 3.3mg
Sodium 576mg
Calcium 159mg

⅓   cup minced green onions
¼   cup tub-style light cream cheese, softened
¼   cup light mayonnaise
¼   cup plain low-fat yogurt
1   teaspoon minced fresh dill
½   teaspoon garlic salt
¼   teaspoon pepper
6   (1½-ounce) French bread rolls
¾   pound cooked peeled large shrimp
1   cup thinly sliced cucumber
½   cup thinly sliced radishes
6   curly leaf lettuce leaves

1. Combine first 7 ingredients in a bowl; stir well.
2. Cut rolls in half horizontally. Spread cream cheese mixture over both sides of rolls; arrange shrimp on bottom halves of rolls. Arrange cucumber and radishes evenly over shrimp; top with lettuce leaves and roll tops. Yield: 6 servings (serving size: 1 sandwich).

Cucumbers: Generally, the smaller the cucumber, the smaller the seeds and the better the flavor. Because cucumbers have a thin skin, they don't require peeling unless they're waxed or if peeling is specified in the recipe. Keep unwashed cucumbers unwrapped in the crisper bin of the refrigerator and away from apples and citrus fruits. These fruits produce ethylene gas that causes the cucumbers to decay.

PHILLY CHEESE SANDWICHES

Next time you want a filling lunch or dinner that requires very little effort,
try these fork-and-knife open-face sandwiches.

1	teaspoon olive oil
1½	cups sliced onion
1½	cups sliced green bell pepper
¼	teaspoon black pepper
4	(1-ounce) slices French or Italian bread

Olive oil-flavored cooking spray

8	ounces thinly sliced deli roast beef
4	(1-ounce) slices reduced-fat Swiss cheese

1. Heat oil in a nonstick skillet over medium heat. Add onion; cook 10 minutes, stirring frequently. Add bell pepper and black pepper; cook 3 minutes or until bell pepper is crisp-tender, stirring frequently.
2. Preheat broiler.
3. Coat top sides of bread slices with cooking spray. Top each slice with 2 ounces beef, ¼ cup onion mixture, and 1 cheese slice.
4. Place sandwiches on a baking sheet; broil 2 minutes or until cheese melts. Yield: 4 servings (serving size: 1 sandwich).

POINTS value:
6

exchanges:
2 starch
2 very lean meat
1 lean meat

per serving:
Calories 291
Fat 8.6g (saturated fat 3.7g)
Protein 24.8g
Carbohydrate 28.4g
Fiber 2.6g
Cholesterol 39mg
Iron 3.2mg
Sodium 819mg
Calcium 365mg

Storing Peppers: Store unwashed, uncut fresh bell peppers in a plastic bag in the refrigerator. They'll keep for about 1 week, depending on how fresh they were when you bought them.

RANCH BURGERS
pictured on page 176

POINTS value:
7

exchanges:
2 starch
1 vegetable
3½ lean meat
½ fat

per serving:
Calories 338
Fat 10.2g (saturated fat 2.7g)
Protein 24.9g
Carbohydrate 35.3g
Fiber 3.4g
Cholesterol 55mg
Iron 4.2mg
Sodium 924mg
Calcium 103mg

Cooking spray
1   cup very thinly sliced green cabbage
½   cup chopped green bell pepper
½   cup chopped onion
1   teaspoon minced fresh or ¼ teaspoon dried oregano
½   teaspoon minced fresh or ⅛ teaspoon dried rosemary
2   tablespoons dry breadcrumbs
2   tablespoons tomato sauce
¾   teaspoon salt
¼   teaspoon black pepper
1   large egg white, lightly beaten
¾   pound ground round
4   (1½-ounce) sesame seed buns, toasted
2   curly leaf lettuce leaves, halved
4   (¼-inch-thick) slices tomato
8   (¼-inch-thick) slices onion
2   tablespoons light ranch dressing

1. Heat a large nonstick skillet coated with cooking spray over medium-high heat. Add cabbage, bell pepper, and onion; sauté 5 to 6 minutes or until tender. Remove from heat; stir in oregano and rosemary. Cool slightly.

2. Combine breadcrumbs, tomato sauce, salt, black pepper, and beaten egg white in a medium bowl. Add cabbage mixture and beef; stir well. Divide mixture into 4 equal portions, shaping each into a ½-inch-thick patty.

3. Prepare grill.

4. Place patties on grill rack coated with cooking spray; grill 5 minutes on each side or until done.

5. Line bottom halves of buns with lettuce leaves; top each with 1 tomato slice, 2 onion slices, and 1 patty. Spoon 1½ teaspoons ranch dressing onto each patty, and cover with tops of buns. Yield: 4 servings (serving size: 1 burger).

CHICKEN–MANGO WRAP

For parties, make an impressive appetizer by slicing these wraps into 2-inch-thick pinwheels. Arrange on a platter, cut sides up.

1	cup diced plum tomato
1	cup diced peeled mango (about 1 medium)
¼	cup diced red bell pepper
¼	cup diced red onion
¼	cup chopped fresh cilantro
3	tablespoons fresh lime juice
1	tablespoon minced seeded jalapeño pepper
⅛	teaspoon salt

Dash of black pepper

8	(7-inch) fat-free flour tortillas
3	cups shredded cooked chicken breast (about 1½ pounds)
½	teaspoon salt
½	cup low-fat sour cream
2	cups thinly sliced red cabbage

POINTS value:
5

exchanges:
1½ starch
1 vegetable
3 very lean meat

per serving:
Calories 245
Fat 3.9g (saturated fat 1.7g)
Protein 20.2g
Carbohydrate 32g
Fiber 2.2g
Cholesterol 50mg
Iron 1.8mg
Sodium 573mg
Calcium 40mg

1. Combine first 9 ingredients in a bowl. Let stand at room temperature 30 minutes.
2. Warm tortillas according to package directions.
3. Combine chicken and ½ teaspoon salt. Spread 1 tablespoon sour cream over each tortilla. Divide chicken evenly among tortillas; top each with ¼ cup mango mixture and ¼ cup cabbage. Roll tortillas over mango mixture, and serve seam side down. Yield: 8 servings (serving size: 1 wrap).

Turkey-Havarti Grinder

Big, bold, and chockablock with turkey, fruit, and cheese, this submarine sandwich for eight is perfect for casual dining and entertaining.

POINTS value:
6

exchanges:
3 starch
1 medium-fat meat

per serving:
Calories 307
Fat 6.9g (saturated fat 1.3g)
Protein 17.1g
Carbohydrate 45g
Fiber 2.6g
Cholesterol 24.8mg
Iron 2.1mg
Sodium 1,094mg
Calcium 98mg

⅓   cup mango chutney
2   tablespoons chopped unsalted, dry-roasted peanuts
2   tablespoons light mayonnaise
Dash of ground red pepper
1   (16-ounce) loaf French bread
1   pound very thinly sliced deli turkey breast
6   curly leaf lettuce leaves
2   ounces thinly sliced reduced-fat Havarti cheese
6   sandwich-cut bread-and-butter pickles
1   Red Delicious apple, cored and sliced into rings

1. Combine first 4 ingredients in a bowl.

2. Cut bread loaf in half horizontally, and spread chutney mixture over bottom half of bread; top with turkey, lettuce, cheese, pickles, apple, and top half of bread. Cut loaf into 8 pieces. Yield: 8 servings (serving size: 1 sandwich).

Chutney: Fruits, vegetables, spices, and vinegars combine in this East Indian condiment to produce a range of flavors. Chutneys of any strength are piquant and flavorful, so a little goes a long way. You can find chutney in the pickle and relish section or jam and jelly section of most supermarkets.

**Wagon Wheel Beef Soup,
page 183**

Spinach Calzones with Blue Cheese,
page 179

Quick Shrimp-and-Corn Soup,
page181

Ranch Burgers, page 170

CAPRI SANDWICH

Serve this flavorful vegetable sandwich with a side of oven fries, and enjoy lemon yogurt with fresh berries for dessert. You may use any ripe black olives instead of the traditional Greek purple-black kalamata olives.

2	teaspoons white wine vinegar
8	(¼-inch-thick) slices tomato (about 2 medium)
1	(16-ounce) loaf French bread
1	garlic clove, halved
1	(1-pound) unpeeled eggplant, cut crosswise into ½-inch slices
4	(¼-inch-thick) slices onion
Cooking spray	
2	tablespoons chopped fresh basil
1	tablespoon chopped kalamata olives
2	(1-ounce) slices provolone cheese, halved

1. Preheat broiler.

2. Drizzle vinegar over tomato slices, and set aside.

3. Slice bread in half horizontally; place, cut sides up, on a baking sheet. Broil 30 seconds or until lightly browned. Rub garlic on cut sides of bread halves; discard garlic.

4. Arrange eggplant and onion slices in a single layer on a baking sheet coated with cooking spray; lightly coat eggplant and onion with cooking spray. Broil 5 minutes; turn slices over, and broil 5 minutes or until lightly browned.

5. Arrange eggplant and tomato on cut side of bottom half of bread. Top with basil and olives, and set aside. Arrange onion slices and provolone cheese on cut side of top half of bread, and broil 30 seconds or until cheese melts. Place on top of bottom half. Cut loaf into 5 pieces. Yield: 5 servings (serving size: 1 sandwich).

POINTS value:
7

exchanges:
3 starch
2 vegetable
½ high-fat meat

per serving:
Calories 349
Fat 7.2g (saturated fat 2.7g)
Protein 12.9g
Carbohydrate 59.3g
Fiber 6.4g
Cholesterol 8mg
Iron 3.3mg
Sodium 719mg
Calcium 177mg

MEDITERRANEAN GOAT-CHEESE SANDWICHES

Fresh-from-the-farm goat cheese and kalamata olive paste lend distinct flavor as a spread for the French bread. Look for olive paste in the condiment section of your grocery store.

POINTS value:
5

exchanges:
2 starch
½ vegetable
1 lean meat

per serving:
Calories 225
Fat 5.2g (saturated fat 2.7g)
Protein 7.8g
Carbohydrate 35.3g
Fiber 1.8g
Cholesterol 15mg
Iron 1.5mg
Sodium 570mg
Calcium 112mg

1	(8–ounce) loaf French bread
½	cup (2 ounces) goat cheese
1	tablespoon kalamata olive paste
1	cup trimmed arugula or fresh spinach
4	(⅛-inch-thick) slices red onion, separated into rings
4	(⅛-inch-thick) slices tomato
6	basil leaves, thinly sliced
½	teaspoon chopped capers
1	teaspoon balsamic vinegar
½	teaspoon olive oil
⅛	teaspoon freshly ground black pepper

1. Slice bread loaf in half horizontally. Spread goat cheese evenly over cut side of bottom half of loaf, and spread olive paste evenly over goat cheese.

2. Layer arugula, onion rings, tomato slices, basil, and chopped capers over olive paste. Drizzle with vinegar and olive oil. Sprinkle with pepper. Place top half of loaf on top. Cut loaf into 4 pieces. Yield: 4 servings (serving size: 1 sandwich).

SPINACH CALZONES WITH BLUE CHEESE

pictured on page 174

We found that a pizza cutter works well for dividing the
refrigerated dough into 4 equal portions.

1 (13.8-ounce) can refrigerated pizza dough
Cooking spray
4 garlic cloves, minced
4 cups baby spinach leaves
8 (⅛-inch-thick) slices Vidalia or other sweet onion
1⅓ cups sliced cremini or button mushrooms
¾ cup (3 ounces) crumbled blue cheese

POINTS value:
8

exchanges:
3 starch
2 vegetable
1 high-fat meat

per serving:
Calories 369
Fat 9.8g (saturated fat 3.8g)
Protein 16g
Carbohydrate 54.2g
Fiber 2.4g
Cholesterol 19mg
Iron 4.2mg
Sodium 988mg
Calcium 186mg

1. Preheat oven to 425°.

2. Unroll dough onto a baking sheet coated with cooking
spray; cut into 4 equal portions. Pat each portion into a 6 x
5-inch rectangle. Sprinkle garlic evenly over rectangles. Top
each rectangle with 1 cup spinach, 2 onion slices, ⅓ cup
mushrooms, and 3 tablespoons cheese. Bring 2 opposite
corners to center, pinching points to seal. Bring remaining
2 corners to center, pinching all points together to seal.
Bake at 425° for 12 minutes or until golden. Yield: 4 servings (serving size: 1 calzone).

Blue Cheese: Whether it's produced from goat's, cow's,
or sheep's milk, a little blue cheese packs a potent punch.
Aging is an important part of the manufacturing of blue
cheese; the longer it's aged, the stronger the flavor. Some of
the blue cheese varieties available in the market include:
Danablu, Gorgonzola, Roquefort, and Stilton.

FALAFEL SANDWICHES

POINTS value:
6

exchanges:
3 starch
1 vegetable
1 fat

per serving:
Calories 312
Fat 8.9g (saturated fat 1.2g)
Protein 12.8g
Carbohydrate 46.7g
Fiber 4.4g
Cholesterol 1mg
Iron 4.3mg
Sodium 536mg
Calcium 181mg

1   (15½-ounce) can garbanzo beans, drained
½   cup chopped onion
¼   cup dry breadcrumbs
1   tablespoon chopped fresh parsley
1   teaspoon ground cumin
½   teaspoon ground coriander
¼   teaspoon salt
⅛   teaspoon black pepper
⅛   teaspoon ground red pepper
2   garlic cloves, peeled and halved
Cooking spray
2   teaspoons olive oil, divided
Tahini Sauce
2   (6-inch) pitas, cut in half
4   curly leaf lettuce leaves

1. Place first 10 ingredients in a food processor, and process until smooth. Divide mixture into 8 equal portions, shaping each into a 2½-inch patty. Coat a large nonstick skillet with cooking spray; add 1½ teaspoons oil, and place over medium-high heat until hot. Add 4 patties to pan; cook 2 minutes on each side or until lightly browned. Repeat procedure with remaining oil and patties.
2. Spread about 2 tablespoons Tahini Sauce evenly into each pita half; fill each half with 1 lettuce leaf and 2 falafel patties. Yield: 4 servings (serving size: 1 sandwich).

Tahini Sauce

½   cup plain fat-free yogurt
2   tablespoons tahini (sesame-seed paste)
1   teaspoon lemon juice
Dash of ground red pepper
1   garlic clove, minced

1. Combine all ingredients in a bowl; stir well with a whisk. Cover and chill, if desired. Yield: ½ cup.

prep: 12 minutes ★ **cook:** 30 minutes

QUICK SHRIMP-AND-CORN SOUP
pictured on page 175

The velvety consistency and rich taste of this soup will make dinner guests think that you worked all day to prepare it.

Cooking spray
1   cup chopped onion
1   cup chopped green bell pepper
1   garlic clove, minced
¾   cup (6 ounces) ⅓-less-fat cream cheese, softened
2   cups fat-free milk
1   (15-ounce) can cream-style corn
1   (10¾-ounce) can condensed reduced-fat, reduced-sodium cream of mushroom soup, undiluted
1   (10-ounce) can diced tomatoes and green chiles, undrained
1¼ pounds medium shrimp, peeled and deveined
4   teaspoons sliced green onions

1. Heat a Dutch oven or large saucepan coated with cooking spray over medium-high. Add chopped onion, bell pepper, and garlic, and sauté 5 minutes. Stir in cream cheese; reduce heat, and cook until cheese is melted. Add milk, corn, soup, and tomatoes; cook 10 minutes, stirring occasionally. Bring to a boil. Add shrimp; cook 5 minutes or until shrimp are done. Remove from heat. Ladle soup into each of 8 bowls. Sprinkle each serving with green onions. Yield: 8 servings (serving size: 1 cup soup and ½ teaspoon green onions).

POINTS **value:**
5

exchanges:
1 starch
2 vegetable
2½ very lean meat

per serving:
Calories 228
Fat 7.4g (saturated fat 3.8g)
Protein 18.8g
Carbohydrate 20.8g
Fiber 1.5g
Cholesterol 118mg
Iron 2.4mg
Sodium 663mg
Calcium 176mg

CHUNKY SOUTHWESTERN CLAM CHOWDER

POINTS value:
6

exchanges:
3 starch
1 lean meat

per serving:
Calories 300
Fat 5.9g (saturated fat 2.8g)
Protein 14.5g
Carbohydrate 50.6g
Fiber 4g
Cholesterol 56mg
Iron 13.6mg
Sodium 476mg
Calcium 137mg

2   red bell peppers (about ¾ pound)
1   jalapeño pepper
1   (10-ounce) can whole clams, undrained
1   bacon slice
1½ cups chopped onion
1½ tablespoons all-purpose flour
4   cups (½-inch) cubed peeled baking potato (about 2 pounds)
2   cups fresh corn kernels (about 4 ears)
1   cup dry white wine or fat-free, less-sodium chicken broth
2   (8-ounce) bottles clam juice
¾   cup half-and-half
½   cup chopped green onions
1   tablespoon chopped fresh basil
¼   teaspoon freshly ground black pepper

1. Preheat broiler.
2. Cut bell peppers in half lengthwise; discard seeds and membranes. Place pepper halves, skin sides up, and jalapeño pepper on a foil-lined baking sheet; flatten bell peppers with hand. Broil 10 minutes or until blackened. Place peppers in a zip-top plastic bag; seal. Let stand 5 minutes. Peel jalapeño, and cut in half; discard seeds and membranes. Chop jalapeño; set aside. Peel and chop bell peppers; set aside. Drain clams in a colander over a bowl; reserve liquid.
3. Cook bacon in a Dutch oven over medium heat until crisp. Remove bacon from pan, reserving drippings in pan. Crumble bacon; set aside. Add chopped onion to pan; sauté 10 minutes. Add flour; cook 2 minutes, stirring constantly. Stir in reserved clam liquid, potato, corn, wine, and bottled clam juice; bring to a boil. Partially cover, reduce heat, and simmer 25 minutes or until potato is tender. Stir in roasted peppers and jalapeño, clams, half-and-half, green onions, basil, and black pepper. Cook 5 minutes or until thoroughly heated. Sprinkle each serving evenly with crumbled bacon. Yield: 6 servings (serving size: 1½ cups).

prep: 5 minutes ★ cook: 24 minutes

WAGON WHEEL BEEF SOUP

pictured on page 173

A handful of pantry staples come together to create this hearty, downhome soup.
Use assorted shapes of pasta and different beans to add variety, or substitute
ground turkey for ground round, if desired.

3	cups uncooked wagon wheel pasta
	Cooking spray
¾	pound ground round
1	cup chopped onion
½	teaspoon dried oregano
1	(1-pound, 10-ounce) bottle low-fat pasta sauce
1	(16-ounce) can red kidney beans, undrained
2	(14-ounce) cans less-sodium beef broth (such as Swanson)

1. Bring 2 quarts water to a boil in a large Dutch oven.
Add pasta, and cook 7 minutes or until done. Drain. Rinse
under cold water; drain and set aside.
2. Coat pan with cooking spray; place over medium-high
heat. Add beef and onion; cook until beef is browned,
stirring to crumble. Drain well, and return beef mixture to
pan. Add cooked pasta, oregano, and remaining ingredients.
Cook over medium-high heat until thoroughly heated.
Yield: 8 servings (serving size: 1½ cups).

***POINTS* value:**
3

exchanges:
1½ starch
½ medium-fat meat

per serving:
Calories 160
Fat 2.9g (saturated fat 1.1g)
Protein 11.2g
Carbohydrate 22.1g
Fiber 3g
Cholesterol 10mg
Iron 2.2mg
Sodium 471mg
Calcium 28mg

SPRING POSOLE

This hearty soup has its roots in Mexico's Pacific Coast region. A combination of pork, hominy, spices, and broth, it's usually a popular holiday meal. Our spring version contains spinach and is topped with the traditional garnishes of chopped lettuce, sliced radishes, and cheese.

POINTS value:
6

exchanges:
1½ starch
2 vegetable
1 lean meat
½ high-fat meat
1 fat

per serving:
Calories 287
Fat 9g (saturated fat 3.7g)
Protein 26g
Carbohydrate 25.9g
Fiber 6.8g
Cholesterol 60mg
Iron 5mg
Sodium 814mg
Calcium 223mg

2	teaspoons olive oil
1	cup chopped onion
2	teaspoons ground cumin
1½	teaspoons ground coriander
¼	teaspoon salt
1	drained canned chipotle chile in adobo sauce, minced
2½	cups diced plum tomato
3	garlic cloves, minced
2	(15.5-ounce) cans golden hominy, rinsed and drained
2	(14-ounce) cans fat-free, less-sodium chicken broth
1	(1-pound) pork tenderloin, trimmed
6	cups chopped fresh spinach
1	cup cilantro leaves
1½	cups thinly sliced romaine lettuce
¾	cup thinly sliced radishes
¾	cup (3 ounces) shredded Monterey Jack cheese
¼	cup thinly sliced green onions

1. Heat oil in a Dutch oven over medium heat. Add chopped onion and next 4 ingredients; sauté 4 minutes. Stir in tomato, garlic, hominy, and broth. Reduce heat, and simmer 20 minutes.

2. Cut pork into bite-size pieces. Add pork, spinach, and cilantro to pan. Cook 7 minutes or until pork is done. Ladle 1½ cups soup into each of 6 bowls; top each with ¼ cup lettuce, 2 tablespoons radishes, 2 tablespoons cheese, and 2 teaspoons green onions. Yield: 6 servings.

CHILE-CHEESE CHOWDER

2	bacon slices
1	cup chopped carrot
1	cup chopped seeded poblano chile (about 3 large)
1	cup chopped onion
2	tablespoons minced seeded jalapeño pepper
½	teaspoon ground cumin
3	garlic cloves, minced
2	(14-ounce) cans fat-free, less-sodium chicken broth
5	cups diced peeled baking potato (1½ pounds)
½	teaspoon salt
⅓	cup all-purpose flour
2½	cups 1% low-fat milk
¾	cup (3 ounces) shredded Monterey Jack cheese with jalapeño peppers
½	cup (2 ounces) shredded reduced-fat sharp Cheddar cheese
⅔	cup sliced green onions

POINTS value:
4

exchanges:
1 starch
1 vegetable
½ lean meat
½ high-fat meat

per serving:
Calories 198
Fat 6.7g (saturated fat 3.9g)
Protein 9.7g
Carbohydrate 25.1g
Fiber 2.5g
Cholesterol 18mg
Iron 1.4mg
Sodium 442mg
Calcium 202mg

1. Cook bacon in a Dutch oven over medium-high heat until crisp. Remove bacon from pan, reserving 1 tablespoon drippings in pan. Crumble bacon; set aside.

2. Add carrot and next 5 ingredients to drippings in pan; sauté 10 minutes or until browned. Stir in broth, scraping pan to loosen browned bits. Add potato and salt. Bring to a boil; cover, reduce heat, and simmer 25 minutes or until potato is tender.

3. Lightly spoon flour into a dry measuring cup; level with a knife. Combine flour and milk in a small bowl, stirring with a whisk. Add to pan. Cook over medium heat 12 minutes or until thick, stirring frequently. Remove from heat. Stir in cheeses. Ladle soup into bowls; top with green onions and crumbled bacon. Yield: 10 servings (serving size: 1 cup soup, about 1 tablespoon green onions, and about 1 teaspoon bacon).

SPINACH-CHICKEN NOODLE SOUP

During the holidays, use leftover turkey instead of chicken in this creamy noodle soup.

POINTS value:
5

exchanges:
1 starch
1 vegetable
2 lean meat

per serving:
Calories 227
Fat 5.9g (saturated fat 1.7g)
Protein 22g
Carbohydrate 18.9g
Fiber 2.3g
Cholesterol 71mg
Iron 2.1mg
Sodium 388mg
Calcium 86mg

4 (14-ounce) cans fat-free, less-sodium chicken broth
1 cup chopped onion
1 cup sliced carrot
2 (10¾-ounce) cans condensed reduced-fat, reduced-sodium cream of chicken soup, undiluted
1 (10-ounce) package frozen chopped spinach, thawed and drained
4 cups chopped cooked chicken
2 cups uncooked medium egg noodles
½ teaspoon salt
½ teaspoon pepper

1. Combine first 3 ingredients in a Dutch oven. Bring to a boil; cover, reduce heat, and simmer 15 minutes. Add cream of chicken soup and remaining ingredients. Bring to a boil; reduce heat, and simmer, uncovered, 15 minutes or until noodles are done. Yield: 8 servings (serving size: 1½ cups).

BUTTERNUT SOUP WITH PEARS AND APPLES

This slightly sweet soup is also delicious topped with plain low-fat yogurt.

1	tablespoon butter
1	cup chopped onion
¾	cup chopped celery
4	cups cubed peeled butternut squash (about 1¼ pounds)
1¾	cups water
1	cup chopped peeled Braeburn or other cooking apple
1	cup chopped peeled Anjou pear
½	cup apple juice
¼	teaspoon salt
⅛	teaspoon pepper
1	(14-ounce) can vegetable broth (such as Swanson)
1	bay leaf
3	tablespoons maple syrup

POINTS value:
2

exchanges:
½ starch
1 fruit
½ fat

per serving:
Calories 117
Fat 2.2g (saturated fat 1.1g)
Protein 1.2g
Carbohydrate 25.5g
Fiber 2.3g
Cholesterol 4mg
Iron 0.8mg
Sodium 402mg
Calcium 48mg

1. Melt butter in a Dutch oven over medium-high heat. Add onion and celery; sauté 4 minutes or until tender. Add squash and next 8 ingredients, and bring to a boil. Partially cover, reduce heat, and simmer 30 minutes or until tender. Discard bay leaf. Place half of squash mixture in a blender or food processor, and process until smooth. Pour puréed mixture into a bowl. Repeat procedure with remaining squash mixture. Return puréed mixture to pan, and stir in syrup. Cook over medium heat 5 minutes or until thoroughly heated. Yield: 7 servings (serving size: 1 cup).

prep: 30 minutes ★ cook: 58 minutes

SUMMER VEGETABLE STEW WITH BASIL PURÉE

pictured on page 156

POINTS value:
5

exchanges:
1 starch
4 vegetable
1½ fat

per serving:
Calories 240
Fat 9.7g (saturated fat 1.7g)
Protein 6.8g
Carbohydrate 35.7g
Fiber 7.5g
Cholesterol 2mg
Iron 3.3mg
Sodium 373mg
Calcium 123mg

1	cup basil leaves
1	garlic clove, peeled and halved
3	tablespoons water
2	tablespoons olive oil
⅛	teaspoon salt
1	tablespoon olive oil
2	bay leaves
1	onion, cut into ¼-inch-thick wedges
6	garlic cloves, peeled and halved
2	thyme sprigs
1½	cups (2-inch-thick) sliced carrots
1	pound small red potatoes, halved
½	teaspoon salt
½	teaspoon black pepper
3	cups (1-inch) cubed yellow squash (about ¾ pound)
1	cup yellow bell pepper strips
½	pound green beans, trimmed and cut into 3-inch pieces
2	tomatoes, peeled and cut into 1-inch pieces
2	tablespoons (½ ounce) shredded fresh Parmesan cheese

1. Place basil and 1 garlic clove in a blender; process until smooth. Add water, 2 tablespoons oil, and ⅛ teaspoon salt; process until blended. Set aside.

2. Heat 1 tablespoon oil in a large Dutch oven over low heat. Add bay leaves; cook 1 minute. Add onion, 6 garlic cloves, and thyme; cover and cook 10 minutes. Add carrot, potato, ½ teaspoon salt, and black pepper; cover and cook 20 minutes. Add squash, bell pepper, and beans; cover and cook 15 minutes. Add tomato; cover and cook 10 minutes. Discard bay leaves and thyme. Ladle 2 cups stew into each of 5 bowls; drizzle each with about 1 tablespoon basil purée, and sprinkle with about 1 teaspoon Parmesan cheese. Yield: 5 servings.

Recipe Index

VEGETABLE COOKING CHART

Vegetable	Servings	Preparations	Cooking Instructions
Asparagus	3 to 4 per pound	Snap off tough ends. Remove scales, if desired.	To steam: Cook, covered, on a rack above boiling water 2 to 3 minutes. To boil: Cook, covered, in a small amount of boiling water 2 to 3 minutes or until crisp-tender.
Broccoli	3 to 4 per pound	Remove outer leaves and tough ends of lower stalks. Wash; cut into spears.	To steam: Cook, covered, on a rack above boiling water 5 to 7 minutes or until crisp-tender.
Carrots	4 per pound	Scrape; remove ends, and rinse. Leave tiny carrots whole; slice large carrots.	To steam: Cook, covered on a rack above boiling water 8 to 10 minutes or until crisp-tender. To boil: Cook, covered, in a small amount of boiling water 8 to 10 minutes or until crisp-tender
Cauliflower	4 per medium head	Remove outer leaves and stalk. Wash. Break into florets.	To steam: Cook, covered, on a rack above boiling water 5 to 7 minutes or until crisp-tender.
Corn	4 per 4 large ears	Remove husks and silks. Leave corn on the cob, or cut off kernels.	Cook, covered, in boiling water to cover 8 to 10 minutes (on cob) or in a small amount of boiling water 4 to 6 minutes (kernels).
Green beans	4 per pound	Wash; trim ends, and remove strings. Cut into 1½-inch pieces.	To steam: Cook, covered, on a rack above boiling water 5 to 7 minutes. To boil: Cook, covered, in small amount of boiling water 5 to 7 minutes or until crisp-tender.
Potatoes	3 to 4 per pound	Scrub; peel, if desired. Leave whole, slice, or cut into chunks.	To boil: Cook, covered, in boiling water to cover 30 to 40 minutes (whole) or 15 to 20 minutes (slices or chunks). To bake: Bake at 400° for 1 hour or until done.
Snow peas	4 per pound	Wash; trim ends, and remove tough strings.	To steam: Cook, covered, on rack above boiling water 2 to 3 minutes. Or sauté in cooking spray or 1 teaspoon oil over medium-high heat 3 to 4 minutes or until crisp-tender.
Squash, summer	3 to 4 per pound	Wash; trim ends, and slice or chop.	To steam: Cook, covered, on a rack above boiling water 6 to 8 minutes. To boil: Cook, covered, in a small amount of boiling water 6 to 8 minutes or until crisp-tender.
Squash, winter (including acorn, butternut, and buttercup)	2 per pound	Rinse; cut in half, and remove all seeds. Leave in halves to bake or peel and cube to boil.	To boil: Cook cubes, covered, in boiling water 20 to 25 minutes. To bake: Place halves, cut sides down, in shallow baking dish; add ½ inch water. Bake, uncovered, at 375° for 30 minutes. Turn and season, or fill; bake 20 to 30 minutes or until tender.